PLEASE RETURN TO THE
CHURCH AT MORGAN HILL
P.O. Box 86, 408/779-1421
Morgan Hill, CA 95037

HEY GOD!

HEY GOD!

Frank Foglio

Edited By
HOWARD G. EARL

Logos International
Plainfield, New Jersey

Unless otherwise identified, all Scriptures are from the King James Version of the Bible.

Library of Congress Catalog Card Number: 72-87328

International Standard Book Number: 0-88270-007-3

Copyright © 1972 by Logos International
All Rights Reserved

Printed in the United States of America

This book is dedicated in love and devotion to my mother for her steadfastness in a life consecrated to Christ; to my loving wife, Julie, for her continuing help and encouragement; to our daughter, Marilyn, and son, Frank, Jr., for their understanding and affection; to one of the greatest men in the Lord I have ever known, Demos Shakarian; and to the Full Gospel Business Men's Fellowship International.

Mamma Foglio

John answered ... I indeed baptize you with water; but one mightier than I cometh, the latchet of whose shoes I am not worthy to unloose: he shall baptize you with the Holy Ghost and with fire.

Luke 3:16

I am come that they might have life, and that they might have it more abundantly.

John 10:10

PUBLISHER'S NOTE

Hey God! is a rollicking story of the Holy Spirit's visitation on an Italian-Catholic family of the previous generation. Its unrefined good humor has already delighted thousands of readers both in the United States and abroad.

Some have noted, however, that misunderstanding might arise among those readers who were unaware that the events recounted in the book occurred during the 1930's. That was a time when charismatic experience seemed of necessity to lead individuals away from their particular denomination. Today, happily, the situation is miraculously different. Many if not most Christians who receive the Baptism of the Holy Spirit no longer find it necessary to seek a new church.

For this, we at Logos praise God. It is not the author's or the Publisher's intention to influence anyone to leave their denomination – on the contrary, we believe the scripture (I Cor. 7:20) that "everyone should remain in the state in which he was called" applies to this case.

Hey God! was written as it happened. Today the author, Frank Foglio, is in great demand as a speaker among all Pentecostals, be they Catholic or Protestant.

Contents

Holy Spirit Baptism

Holy Spirit Baptism

Through the power of Jesus Christ, we can be healed in many ways. He can heal our bodies, our minds, our finances, our marriages, our relationships with others, our employment problems, and many other plagues which tear us apart as individuals and families. I learned this many years ago, and since then I can truthfully say that nothing shakes me, nothing bothers me, and nothing distracts me—as long as His anointing is on me.

I am reminded of the latter part of Luke 5:17: "And the power of the Lord was present to heal them." And that wonderful affirming statement in Phil. 4:13: "I can do all things through Christ which strengtheneth me." The healing and the strengthening through the power of Christ gives us power that we never dreamed possible for us to possess. I am certain of that. I have seen it demonstrated in my life, first when I was a twelve-year-old boy.

We lived in the western hills of Pennsylvania, in the sizable community of Burgettstown, until I was nine years old. My brothers—Joseph, Costy, Carmen, George, and Anthony—and I were born there, as were two of my sisters, Dolly and Jessie. One day in 1925, my dad came home from the Pennsylvania Railroad roundhouse where he worked and announced to Mamma that we were going to move.

Mamma began to cry and fuss because moving meant she would leave all her Roman Catholic Italian neighbors. Dad usually called her Mamma except when he became especially stern; then he addressed her as Angelina. Her maiden name was Angeline Crede Dio; Crede Dio interpreted in English means "believe in God." Mamma believed in God according to Roman Catholic teaching, and she did not want to leave a neighborhood of Italians with like beliefs. She used this argument in remonstrating with Dad to remain in Burgetts-town. But James Foglio, called "Little Jim" by fellow workers, became adamant.

"Angelina," he said, "for many a month something has a been telling me to get out to the country. I don't understand it. I know we're gonna move. I've rented a farm for ten dollars a month five miles from here. It's in the Racoon School District."

That was a long speech for Dad, who could neither read nor write. But he could bargain. He rented a ninety-five-acre farm with a big house and barns and acreage laden with fruit trees and big patches of blackberries, strawberries, and rasp-berries. He had persuaded the Raccoon School District prin-cipal to rent him the farm for the ridiculously low price on the promise that he would keep the farm in tip-top shape.

Despite all the advantages Dad enumerated, Mamma still cried and fussed about leaving the area where her children's godmothers and godfathers lived. Dad said, "We're *gonna move.*" And we did.

We were on the farm only a few weeks when Dad stopped a black man going by and asked him to have dinner with us. He did, and Dad made a deal with him. Slim Hopper was to plow our land for very little pay in actual money but plenty of farm produce plus fruits and berries. Slim agreed, and soon afterward his wife appeared on the scene. A beautiful, tall black woman with a pleasant voice, Mrs. Hopper displayed a certain quality of peace that made her different from anyone we had ever known.

She agreed to help Mamma with the children and also help clean the house and cook, if Dad would let her use a parcel of land of her own choosing for a garden. Dad agreed, and she walked over most of the farm, stopping occasionally to bow

14

her head and then look heavenward. She came back toward the house and stopped at a plot of land beside a brook. She stood with bowed head for a few minutes, then looked up to heaven and said something. She returned to the house.

"I'll take that parcel over by the brook," she said.

"You crazee, woman. That's bad ground. No grow nothing. Not even weeds."

"I'll take it," she answered.

That plot out-produced any other land on Dad's farm. He couldn't understand it. The next year Dad told her he wanted that parcel for a special reason, and she would have to select another plot. She went through the same procedure as before and finally made her decision. And wouldn't you know, *that* land produced abundantly beyond any other plot of ground on the farm. Dad couldn't understand it. Neither could we.

The second year on the farm we were a family of twelve: a brother, Fred, and sister, Yolanda, were born, making ten children and Mamma and Dad. We were a devout Roman Catholic family—all except Dad, who was an agnostic. He believed only in himself. We served our religion with our whole mind, body, and soul. That was all we knew. We held it dear to our hearts. We respected the saints, we kept the saints' days, and we knew assurance. We were guaranteed absolutely that we were saved. No matter what, we could make it to heaven. And we believed it. We were sincere in our beliefs, but evidently that wasn't good enough for God. He had a different plan for our salvation, different from the one we were living.

God revealed His plan to us one Sunday afternoon in a mighty moving way. We were at home, waiting for the spaghetti to cook. That's an exciting time in an Italian's life—the pot is on the stove, the spaghetti is boiling, and the sauce is good. Then is no time to postpone serving the meal for which the family has been waiting all morning and into the afternoon. But disturbances were the order of that day.

It started with a knock on our door. Before anyone had a

chance to reach the door, it flew open, and twelve strangers walked into our house. Each one carried a little black book. We didn't know them, and they didn't know us, but they introduced themselves real fast. They were the Montecalvos, another Italian family like our own; a mother and father and ten children. They said they had been baptized in the Holy Spirit, and God had directed them to seek us out, although they did not know our names. They had come many miles to teach us—the Foglio family—the Word of God.

The little black book each Montecalvo carried was a copy of the New Testament, the book which we, as Catholics, were forbidden to read. We were members of Our Lady of Lourdes Church, a wonderful Roman Catholic Church. But Father McCashin said we were not to read that little black book. He said, "If you want to know anything about it, bring it to me. I'll read it. I'll interpret it, and I'll keep it for you."

What were we to do? Here we were, trapped by this sudden invasion of our home. There was no escape. The Montecalvo boys grabbed my brothers and me. The girls began to deal with my sisters. Their mother dealt with my mother. No one touched my dad, who was four-feet-eleven and one of the meanest men I have ever known. He had no fear of anything. In fact, fear was a word completely out of his vocabulary. He cursed God. He cursed the angels. He cursed the saints. He cursed the priests personally. He cursed the pope, and he cursed the devil. He cursed everyone and everything. When there was no one else upon whom to spew forth his venom, he focused it upon his wife and children. The devil didn't want him, and I guess, neither did the Lord. He had his own religion, which was hating everything and everybody.

When those people invaded our home, my dad's mind hit upon a single thought: they were trespassing. That gave him the right to load the double-barreled shotgun and really work them over. He started for the corner of the room where he cached his firearms, reached there ahead of my mother who understood his intentions, and grabbed the shotgun. My mother caught hold of him as he picked up the weapon.

These invaders with the Word of God were not afraid of my dad, shotgun or no. They ignored him like a barking dog without teeth. He cursed them. He said things an unsaved individual never would think of saying. The Montecalvos merely ignored him completely and continued telling us about Jesus, and reading from their little black books.

"You must be born again," they said. "You must be filled with the Holy Spirit. You must be baptized by immersion. You only got sprinkled."

They didn't soft-pedal anything. They told us about Jesus Christ, the crucifixion, the risen Savior. They said Christ is very much alive today. Mary is a wonderful woman, but she does not overshadow Jesus Christ. She is not greater than our Lord and Savior. God used her. The Holy Immaculate Conception brought forth Jesus, the Christ. They were sold on what they were preaching, and they were smart.

It was the first time in the history of the Foglio family that the kids had nothing to say. How could you talk back when you didn't know what the other family was talking about? What's the Holy Ghost? We had heard of ghosts flying around, wrapped in white sheets. What's speaking in tongues? We talk in Italian and English. We didn't need to learn any other language. What's assurance of heaven and going to heaven? We had that. No matter what we did, a little penance and we were on our way; go to confession, straighten it all out, and be worse the following week.

We didn't want any new religion. We didn't want to hear anything else. But that family was so well-versed in the Word and anointed with the power of the Holy Spirit of God that we *had* to listen. There was something about them and the way they explained the Word that held our attention like a giant vise grips a piece of steel. We couldn't argue when we had no ammunition with which to refute what was being said. And so, we just sat there like mutes. We could hear, but we couldn't talk back, as they explained the salvation plan through the redemptive power of Jesus Christ. They were so excited, so sold on Christ, that we couldn't do a thing except hunger for more of the Word.

My mother was the first and only one to regain her ability to speak, to defend the religious beliefs of her little family. With the rosary clutched in her hand, she said, "Just a minute!" She also was four-feet-eleven.

"Just a minute! Hold on! Don't try to pour this crazy religion down our throats. Don't tell me our way isn't the only way."

"No!" they said. "It isn't."

"Well, don't tell me I'm wrong."

"Yes! You are wrong."

Mother said, "Don't you criticize Mary, the Mother of God."

"She isn't the Mother of God."

These people had just plain guts. They spoke up for what they believed and had no qualms about disputing the beliefs of a devout Roman Catholic. But my mother wasn't backing down either.

"Don't forget," she said, "you've talked about Saint Peter. He was our first pope. Don't you dare even mention his name."

I never saw my mother mad in her life. She was always a meek, scared, shaky thing. Dad beat her up once a week, just to let her know he was around. But suddenly she is defending her little family, defending that which she believes. That's good. Praise God! You and I are going to have to give an accounting very soon. That which we believe is going to be sorely tried. Don't relax. Don't think you are going to sprout wings, fly away, and miss it all. You are going to see the main feature, and you had better have your faith strong enough for the test.

My mother's faith was invincible as the battle with the Montecalvos raged in our home. She accused them of belittling the saints, the popes, and the beliefs of the Roman Catholic Church. The Montecalvos held steadfast to their beliefs, also, and they had the Holy Spirit with them for extra power. Finally the mother of the Montecalvos motioned everyone to silence and then she took off.

"Now, all of you listen," she said. "I'm going to tell you exactly the way it is. First, the *only* way to God is through Jesus Christ, His Son. Second, the so-called Mother of God, Mary. I'll t⌐˙ you something about her. She was a wonderful woman. Go˙ used her. She conceived Christ by the Holy Spirit. Now, let me read from the New Testament what happened on the Day of Pentecost in the Upper Room." She read the version from Acts 2:1-4: "And when the day of Pentecost was fully come, they were all with one accord in one place. And suddenly there came a sound from heaven as of a rushing mighty wind, and it filled all the house where they were sitting. And there appeared unto them cloven tongues like as of fire, and it sat upon each of them. And they were all f˙led with the Holy Ghost, and began to speak with other ˙ ngues, as the Spirit gave them utterance."

She stopped reading, and before anyone had an opportunity to say anything, she explained, "They were in the Upper Room when this happened. Read Acts 1:13,14. It says, 'They went up into an upper room, where abode both Peter, and James, and John, and Andrew, Philip, and Thomas, Bartholomew, and Matthew, James the son of Alphaeus, and Simon Zelotes, and Judas the brother of James. These all continued with one accord in prayer and supplication, with the women, and Mary the mother of Jesus, and with His brethren.' "

We had never heard of the Upper Room. But we were listening with mouths agape, holding on to each word as though it were a shining jewel that we did not want to escape us. While we were still in stunned silence, Mrs. Montecalvo smiled ever so sweetly at my mother and said, "I am glad you mentioned Peter, your first pope. You see, by the Word of God, he was one of the first Pentecostals. A Holy Roller, like you folks call us. So was Mary, the mother of Jesus."

While their mother was talking, the Montecalvo children were showing my sisters, brothers, and me what their mother had read from the little black book. We couldn't deny it. It was right there in the Word of God.

"Oh!" I thought. "Mary, the Mother of God, she also received the baptism in the Holy Spirit. And she probably danced all over the Upper Room. Mary! Mary, whom we always saw with the little baby Jesus in her arms."

My mother said, "Mary! She, too, is like you people? Humph! How tragic!"

Total strangers had come into our home, established a beachhead and proceeded to knock over our sand castles. With the love of God and His anointing on their lives, they disarmed us completely. We had no defense. We couldn't defend ourselves, because we didn't know what it was all about.

When they had finished telling us about Jesus Christ and the plan of salvation through His redeeming power, they employed a piece of incomparable strategy.

"Let us pray," they said.

Let us *pray?* How sneaky can you get? You can't say no to a suggestion of prayer if you claim to be a professing Christian. They knelt down. There was nothing for us to do but to kneel, also. So, we did. Now, you might think that we would close our eyes to pray. But we didn't; we wanted to see what they would do next. How did we know but that they might take off and fly around the room?

While they prayed, they made funny noises under their breath, as though they were whispering some mumbo-jumbo language. My dad raged back and forth across the room, cursing and calling God and everyone names. And during that prayer, something happened that touched my heart. The old gentleman, the father of the Montecalvos, the one who led the pack to our home, raised his eyes heavenward and stretched out his arms to God and said, "Oh, God, forgive them. Oh,

God, open their minds and their hearts. Let the love of Christ saturate them. God, let them see their lost condition. Let them know that they are alienated from Thee. Oh, God, we love them. God, let them understand." Tears flowed down his cheeks.

Such compassion! Such love! He didn't even know us, and yet he wept for us. Something happened to me. As a little boy, hardly twelve years old, I felt a change come into my life. Something had touched me. It made me feel good, like jumping into a cool, refreshing pool of water on a hot summer day. I felt clean and refreshed all over.

The Montecalvos finished their prayer with a loud "Amen" and were gone, leaving with us twelve of their little black books. My mother had taken about all she could. She spun around and ran up a stairway of seventeen steps, slamming the door behind her. We could hear her up in her bedroom. She was mad at God. She did not pray. She shouted at God.

"Hey God! Look! God, You listen to me. Do You mean to tell me all these years I've been wrong?"

The Foglios were lined up in the living room at the entrance to the stairway, and although the door leading to the stairway was closed, we could hear the commotion.

"God! Do You mean to tell me all these years I've led my family wrong? God!" She was beating the floor with her fists. "God! Is it so what they said? I must be born again? I must have the baptism in the Holy Spirit? And make funny noises like those people made when they were praying?"

My mother was right. They did make the funniest noises when they prayed. They didn't speak English. They didn't speak Italian. They spoke another language. We didn't understand it.

Up in that bedroom my mother still was talking to God. "Hey God! If I must receive the baptism in the Holy Spirit, I want it now. I want You, God, to give it to me right now." She stopped speaking. The next instant it seemed there were a hundred people up there. My mother had her own Upper

Room. It no longer sounded like a tiny woman alone. We could hear her making those funny noises and carrying on.

I thought, "Oh, my God, she has torn all her clothes to shreds. She's ripped her hair out by the roots. Yes, she has." The noises she was making, the pounding and beating on the floor, I was certain, could be heard throughout the house.

I don't know why I tried to be a hero. I thought I had better go up and check on Mamma. I grabbed hold of the doorknob leading to the stairway, pulled the door open about two feet, and there was a mighty rushing wind going up that stairway and into Mamma's bedroom and back down the stairway again. It caught hold of the door, ripped it out of my hand, and slammed it shut. There wasn't a breeze blowing anywhere outside or inside, except in that stairway and Mamma's bedroom. When that door slammed shut, the Foglio children turned pure white. We knew something supernatural was happening, and we were afraid. Boy, were we frightened!

We waited. Soon we heard Mamma coming down the stairway. We stopped breathing. What was going to come out of that doorway? Finally the door opened, and Mamma stepped into the living room. We never had seen her look so beautiful. A glow surrounded her. And I never saw anyone look so silly in all my life. She had a grin from ear to ear and was rocking on her heels. She went up to Dad and tried to talk, but all that came from her mouth were those funny noises.

Dad said, "Ah, she's crazee. She's crazee. We lost our Mamma. She's crazee." He backed away from her.

Mamma continued grinning, and Dad kept backing away. She couldn't speak in English or Italian, only the queer mumbo-jumbo language of the Montecalvos. We Roman Catholic Italian children watched her, all of us, scared to death. Dad just didn't want anything to do with her. He wasn't afraid. She walked into the kitchen and took a long look at the old coal-burning cookstove. Those were bad times. We couldn't afford a better stove. We were so poor that the poor people called us poor.

The stove was red hot. The coffeepot, the spaghetti, the sauce, and the water should have been boiling over. But they weren't. Mamma stood there, looking over the situation, grinning and rocking on her heels. I guess she saw an angel stirring the spaghetti. She came into the living room, grinned at everyone, and went up to her room again to another session with probably a hundred angels. Finally, she came down. This time she preached a sermon to us.

"Family, this is it," she said. "This is real. This is of God. And now I'm going to tell you about Jesus."

Every time she got close to us we would have to back away. The biggest coward in the whole family suddenly had become commander in chief. We could feel the power emanating from her, and her face still held that radiant glow.

"Those people were right," she said. "God spoke to me, and He told me so. We will have to mend our ways. Our whole way of life must change. I will show you. I will lead you to God through Jesus Christ, our Lord and Savior."

She set the table for dinner. We had a big table. It could seat eighteen. Dad built it with one-by-twelve planks—a big table for a big family—and our door was always open to everyone, regardless of who came by; Catholic or Protestant, black or white, they were invited to come in and eat with us.

We were hungry by the time Mamma had the food on the table. It was early evening, and we had spent most of the afternoon listening to that invading family and then the sessions with Mamma.

Once seated at the Foglio table, with the food on, everyone grabs for something. You can't afford to waste any time with so many kids vying for food, along with Mamma and Dad. But this evening no one grabbed. We started to when—

"Hold it!" Mamma ordered. "Just a minute. Nobody touch nothing. I'm gonna pray."

She prayed for half an hour for us sinners. Then, when that was finished, she was all choked up and began the mumbo-jumbo language of the Montecalvos, which lasted for twenty minutes. "Chal ma kei a mumba kaio."

"What's all that noise, anyway?" I wondered. Dad was right. "She's crazee." It was a shame, but something did happen to her in her own Upper Room.

That was the hardest meal the Foglio family ever ate. We could hardly swallow it. We didn't know what Mamma would do next, and we were watching her instead of eating.

Bedtime that night was something I will never forget. My brother George and I slept in one room on the second floor with our brothers and sisters on the same floor in rooms opening off a circular hallway. Below, Mamma would walk around underneath our bedrooms as she recited the Rosary or read out of a prayer book to us. We went to sleep with her soothing voice the last sound of which we were conscious each night. But this evening was different.

Mamma had a booming voice, something unusual, I guess, for a small woman. But it had a certain pleasant resonance. She stood underneath the room in which George and I slept. "Hey God," she said. "You see George. You see Frank. You see them up there."

We could feel God's finger right in the middle of our backs. "Give them what I got, God," she said. Around and around she went underneath each room, asking God to give each one of her children what she had received. Finally, she came underneath the room where she and Dad slept. She said nothing. For what seemed almost a minute, there was complete silence, and then everything broke loose up in that room over her head.

Dad took his shoe and began to beat it on the floor. "Ah, you crazee. Say something. I know you're down there. Say something. You crazee."

Curiosity overpowered me, so I went downstairs on the pretense of wanting a glass of water. Mamma was ready to shoo me back upstairs, when a knock came on the door. It was Mrs. Hopper after some milk. Mamma was so happy over her baptism in the Holy Spirit she had to tell Mrs. Hopper about it.

"Praise the Lord! I know all about it," she explained. "I don't do nothing without praying. God guides me even to selecting garden plots. I pray over them, and they produce abundantly."

"Why didn't you tell me?" Mamma asked.

"Honey, you would not have accepted or understood. I had to pray to God that He would send someone to tell you, and He sent the Montecalvos all the way from Pennsylvania. Praise the Lord!"

Mother leaped up and threw her arms around Mrs. Hopper, and they had a hallelujah time. I understood now why Mrs. Hopper's gardens produced more than Dad's. But there were more and greater surprises in the days and weeks ahead.

Fearless Witnessing for Christ

Fearless Witnessing for Christ

We did not know what Mamma was going to do next. Every order, every command she gave was with sparkling eyes and a big smile. She had received a new charisma that you just could not resist. She was just full of something that we did not understand.

The morning after receiving her baptism, Mamma was waiting for us when we came down from our bedrooms. Immediately after breakfast the blow struck. "All right, kids," she said. "I want you to bring every magazine, every book, and every phonograph record that doesn't glorify God. Bring everything here."

We didn't know what she intended to do with such a collection. Maybe she wanted to bless them. We soon discovered just how much Mamma knew about what was going on around our house. She knew where every magazine, book, and record was hidden: under the rug, under a mattress, and in the barn. She knew. And we brought them to her.

We carried everything outside and started a bonfire, then stood back watching the flames devour all our prized possessions.

After the final licking flames had subsided to glowing embers, Mamma gathered her brood and took us into the house where new surprises awaited. She had every bench, every chair—anything upon which a body could sit—brought into the living room and lined up in neat rows like church pews. We did it without questioning her.

"All right," she said, standing back and surveying the living room with a look of satisfaction. "Now all of you go into Burgettstown. Go to the homes of your godmothers and god-fathers and their families." You better believe a big Italian family in those days had plenty of these kinds of relatives. Before I finished the thought, Mamma was talking again. "Tell them that Mrs. Foglio is going to have a big feast tonight at seven-thirty. They're all invited."

It still was early morning with a long day ahead, and even at my youthful age, I knew when you told an Italian you were going to have a feast, he began to fast. At least, it was so in those days. You could guarantee he wouldn't eat a thing all day long. My brothers and sisters and I went into Burgetts-town and invited seventy-eight to the feast.

I kept a sharp watch on Mamma throughout the rest of the day, after returning home. It's a wonder this poor little Ital-ian boy didn't have an ulcer. I could see Mamma wasn't cooking a thing. What feast did she mean? In those days, an Italian feast lasted several days. Mamma hadn't prepared any ravioli, lasagna, spaghetti, or salami. Nothing! She hadn't even brought out the bread. What feast? I didn't get it. Five o'clock came, and then six. Still nothing to indicate a feast was being prepared. Mamma certainly was going to have to work a miracle and do it in a hurry.

Seven o'clock! The guests started arriving. They came with their pipes and cigars and big smiles, full of anticipation. They looked around. No food! They began sniffing for the odor of food. They had a good sense of smell. In fact, there is a story among Italians that when in a strange town and look-ing for a restaurant, an Italian will put his head out of a car window and he can smell a restaurant a mile away. But there was no food odor in our home.

I said to myself, "My God, what might happen here tonight when they learn there is no feast? I don't know what Mamma had planned, but anything could happen. They could trample Mamma to death—and us, too. Seventy-eight hungry, unsaved Italians—and nothing is more dangerous than an

unsaved Italian who is hungry. Why, they probably will bar-
becue us."

I prayed, "Oh, my God! You had better do something
here. Oh, Mary, Mother of God, help us." Mamma had us
herd the guests into the living room. They sat in chairs and
on benches and stools we had arranged in rows.

Mamma came into the room. I have never seen such courage in all my life. She was smiling and bowing, and that big
grin stretched from ear to ear. She was holding something
behind her back. I looked. That little black book! That did it
for me. I took a seat right in the front row by the door where
I could be the first one out and really go. My sisters were
biting their fingernails down to the first knuckles, they were
so scared.

Mamma said, "I promised you a feast, and you gonna have
a feast. I'm gonna tell you about Jesus."

I said, "Lord Jesus and Mother Mary, help us. Saint
Anthony and Saint Christopher, where are you?"

I heard nothing except Mamma preaching. I looked
around, and seventy-eight Italians were paralyzed. Their
mouths gaped open, and their eyes grew bigger than the pro-
verbial saucers. I noticed one man. A lighted cigar fell out of
his mouth, dropped on his leg, and burned through his trousers, and he never moved. Mamma told them about Jesus,
about the joy and peace she had found. Then she went into
those funny noises.

I said, "This will do it." But it didn't. The guests turned
pure white. They did not move. Pipes were on the floor.
Partially smoked cigars were clutched between fingers. When
Mamma finished talking, she used the strategy she had
learned from the family who told us about Jesus. She said,
"Now, let's pray."

I said, "This will do it. Now watch the chairs fly! They'll
go out the windows!" But it didn't happen that way.

Everyone knelt down and Mamma prayed. She prayed for
seventy-eight sinners plus the eleven unsaved in her family. I

began to hear some sobbing in a corner. Then I heard someone sobbing on the other side of me and behind me and all around me. These people were crying. When Mamma said, "Amen," they got to their feet. There wasn't a dry eye among those seventy-eight people.

Mamma asked, "How you like the feast?"

They wanted to know, "When are we going to have another?"

That was Mamma's first prayer meeting. She held one every week for thirty-nine years, and there was not a person who attended the first prayer meeting who was not saved eventually—saved and filled with the Holy Spirit.

Mamma began judging everything by "What saith the Word?" When a problem developed, she'd say, "Just a minute!" Then she would flip the pages of the Bible. "Ah! Here! Hear what saith the Word of God." She began running our home, our lives, according to the Word of God.

My dad grew worse and worse. No more talking. Nothing. He slept on the floor every night for three months. He was afraid to get into bed with Mamma. I saw him once when he was about to hit her. He stopped. He was afraid he would pull back a stump instead of a hand. He wouldn't go near her. He wouldn't touch her. Even he respected God's anointed.

One day while reading the Bible, Mamma was inspired to take up a visitation mission, visiting the homes in Italian neighborhoods in nearby towns to tell the families about Jesus, just as the Montecalvo family witnessed to us.

"Come on, kids. You come along with Mamma."

Two or three of us would go with her from door to door in Italian neighborhoods. Imagine taking Catholic children along with her to witness. On our first mission, we walked five or six miles to get to the first house in the nearest town. The population was 75 percent Catholic, and Mamma was a little woman. But she was anointed with the power of the Holy Spirit and did a mighty work.

Father McCashin looked out over his congregation one

Sunday morning at the first Mass and saw seven rows of empty pews. He bellowed, "What goes on here?" First time anyone ever heard him speak a word in English. "Where are the Foglios? Where are the Sarracinos and the Bonis?"

The good priest had preached to big families. Every time a mother and dad were saved, the whole family joined the church, which meant twelve, thirteen, fourteen, or fifteen children. We had a new Sunday-school class every time a family was saved.

One of the parishioners stood up and told the priest, "The Holy Rollers are taking our families." The priest lost no time in laying down rules for countering the attack. He told the congregation, "When these people come to your home, don't listen to them. Close your ears. Don't let them into your homes. Hit them with anything at hand. Don't even open the door."

That was the kind of resistance Mamma ran into the next day when she headed for an Italian neighborhood. She was leading the pack. Two of my sisters were with her, and I was dawdling along about twenty-five feet in the rear. Mamma knocked on the door of a white clapboard house. I saw the curtain to the window by the door pulled aside, and a big woman looked out through the window. She looked vicious. The next instant, she pulled the door open and stood there with a bucket of hot water. The way the steam was rising from it, I could tell the water was scalding. I knew immediately what she had in mind, because the look on her face didn't indicate love. But Mamma had a way of disarming people. She smiled sweetly and said hello.

"What do you want?"

"I want to tell you about Jesus."

"Tell me and tell me quickly."

Mamma told the woman about Jesus and His love. She told her about God, the plan of salvation; how she felt, the joy she received from knowing and loving Jesus. That woman set her bucket down before Mamma was more than halfway through talking, and by the time Mamma finished, the woman was crying and wiping away the tears with her apron.

Mamma said, "You had better scrub your floors before the water gets cold." She grabbed Mamma, hugged her and said, "You know, I was going to throw it on you."

Mamma knew that. She wasn't afraid. She had a Holy Ghost anointing on her life. After she turned that town upside down, she decided to go to another one, Steubenville, Ohio. At that time the Italian area in Steubenville was so bad that the people were afraid to go out at night. The people in that neighborhood were so violent that even the dogs wouldn't walk the streets after dark. Mamma was warned not to go there.

"The Lord told me to go and I'm going."

Mamma usually witnessed in a neighborhood by starting with the first house in the block and working her way down one side of the street and up the other. One day when she was visiting one particular block, I didn't feel like going along. My two sisters, Jessie and Yolanda, went with her. They approached a house in the middle of the block, and Mamma knocked on the door. Immediately the door opened, and standing there, filling the doorframe, was a six-foot-seven man who weighed around 240 pounds.

"Come in!" he commanded them.

They walked inside, and he slammed the door shut and leaned his back against it. He had an eighteen-inch butcher knife in his hand. He jammed it against Mamma's stomach. She felt the blade against her flesh.

"Now see if your Jesus can save you, because I'm going to kill you and your daughters." The man had made the threat without knowing whether Mamma and my sisters knew Jesus. There had been no time to mention Jesus before the threat was uttered. He had to be demon-possessed to have such knowledge. Mamma didn't know then, but we learned later that the whole neighborhood feared this man. He had been watching Mamma and my two sisters through the window in his living room, watching every move they made, and he couldn't wait for them to get to his door so that he might order them inside and kill them. That was his plan.

He was pressing the butcher knife against Mamma's flesh. My sisters were panic-stricken. But Mamma just smiled as if the knife wasn't there.

"I want to tell you about Jesus."

"Tell it and be quick about it, because you're gonna die."

She told him about Jesus in as few words as she could, and when she stopped talking, he asked, "You finished?"

"Just one more favor I want from you."

"What's that?"

"Before you kill me, I like to pray."

"All right, pray. But make it short."

She knelt down on both knees, and he held the knife's point between her shoulders. (Could you pray in such a situation? There will come a day just exactly like that. Can you pray with a bayonet between your shoulders? The day will come, and you had best be prepared to meet it.)

"Hey God! You know he dunno what he do. Look at him, God. You love him. You gave Your son to die for him. If he was the only man alive, God, You would still give Your Son. Lord, bless him. Lord, deliver him. Lord, I love him. Even if he kills me, Lord, I still love him."

The knife clattered to the floor. The man fell on his face and wrapped his arms around Mamma's ankles, and he wouldn't let go.

"I am being prayed through," he cried. "Saved, healed, and delivered. Healed by the Holy Spirit and the power of God."

He stood up, grabbed Mamma and my two sisters and hugged them until he almost broke them in two. God had a reason for saving that man; he became a bodyguard for Mamma and her flock.

"Whenever you come into this neighborhood from now on," he said, "let me go with you to protect you."

God continued to give that man, healed by the Holy Spirit, vicious eyes. He would be testifying before a group and crying, but his eyes shone like twin pieces of carbon steel. All the hate over the years had left its scars, but he had the joy of the Lord in his heart. Mamma and my sisters would call at his home, and he would take his little black book and go with them to other homes. He would knock on a door, and whoever answered it saw this huge man standing there.

"What would you like? Huh!"

"My friends want to tell you about Jesus. Okay?"

Who is going to argue with a man who nearly fills the doorway? "Oh, yes. Come in. Please do."

Many listened and were convicted and baptized in the Holy Spirit. They started a large prayer meeting in that town which later developed into a church, a wonderful testimony of what one small woman can do for her Lord and Savior when she dares to believe. Mamma was stoned in some towns, but she refused to be intimidated as she continued with her work. Her faith and fearlessness in witnessing reminds me of Acts 4:29: "And now, Lord, behold their threatenings: and grant unto thy servants, that with all boldness they may speak the word."

Jesus tells us that "a prophet is without honor in his own home." This was true with the mother of the Foglio brood. Her husband and her children were laggards when it came to conversion to her faith. I was the first in the family to accept Mamma's teaching and be infilled with the Holy Spirit. That baptism was so wonderful. I didn't know how to receive it. I thought the Lord would come into the room with me and that would be it. He would just walk into the room, lay His hands on me, and I would be infilled with the Holy Spirit. For many mornings I said, "This is the day." But nothing happened. I believed. I was sincere.

Each morning I said under my breath, "Hurry up, Lord. Touch me now." But God will not be rushed. He says, "Be still, and know that I am God" (Ps. 46:10). And again, "Have no anxiety about anything, but in everything by prayer and supplication with thanksgiving let your requests be made known to God" (Phil. 4:6 RSV).

I did not know then that such gems of advice were in the Bible, because I was new in reading the Holy Scripture. Neither did I understand that sometimes the Lord delays in answering prayer for our own good. He may be delaying because He has something better awaiting us, but we are not yet prepared to receive it.

I stopped pleading with God to hurry my baptism. I began to say, "I know, God, You will touch me. You will fill me with the Holy Spirit. Thank You, God."

One morning shortly after I was twelve years old, I knelt alone in my bedroom and said, "Jesus come into my heart and take over my life."

It happened with the quickness of streaked lightning in a summer, storm-clouded sky. I felt God's hand between my shoulder blades. A sweet presence like fine rain went from the top of my head to the bottoms of my feet. Shower after shower of the blessings of God came forth. I spoke in other tongues. I was under the power of God for two weeks. I couldn't get away from that power, could not shut it off. Someone merely had to say "Jesus," and I was on my way.

I became so hungry for the Word. It was better than eating good food. I carried the New Testament in my pocket into my classrooms in school. During a study period, I would put the little black book between the pages of my big geography book which I stood upright on my desk. Those geography books were so massive that any ordinary book could be hidden by them.

One day I was reading about the Acts of the Apostles. It was good and growing progressively better. I became so involved that I actually was walking and conversing with those men of God. I forgot that I was in school. My environment had been transplanted thousands of miles away to the land of the early Christians. Suddenly I felt filled to overflowing with the Holy Spirit.

"Ako makei asundra ma heika!" I shouted.

The sound of my voice shattered the spell, returned me to the geography book, the desk, and the schoolhouse. The outburst shook that schoolroom. Students were looking anxiously about, wondering what might happen next. The principal was standing directly behind me. He could see the New Testament concealed between the pages of that big book. He saw this little Italian fellow reading the Bible and heard the funny noises he made.

All the boys, and men too, in those days wore suspenders. Without uttering a word, the principal reached down and with two fingers grabbed my suspenders between the shoulder blades, stretched the rubber suspenders back about four feet and let go. When they snapped against my back, I jumped straight up toward the ceiling.

"Hallelujah!" I shouted. I thought I had been translated.

The principal did not say a word. No one said anything. I had scared the class and the teacher and had shaken the principal. He walked out of the room. No one ever mentioned the episode to me. I thought afterward that if the principal had snapped my suspenders any harder, I *would* have gone through the ceiling. My mind was so fixed on the apostles that I had lost all sense of earthly reality, all sense of anyone or anything about me.

An Empty Gas Tank

An Empty Gas Tank

I thank God for my wonderful Christian mother and for the Holy Spirit filled Montecalvo family who brought the light of truth to her. I praise God that Mamma withstood the onslaughts of that invading family until she could get alone with God and thresh the whole matter out with Him. I think this unwillingness, to the point of unswerving determination, on Mamma's part, showed her strength of character. She was not a wishy-washy woman. Once she became convinced by God and had the baptism in the Holy Spirit, there was no holding her. She became a true disciple of Christ, witnessing for her Lord wherever circumstances located her.

God moved mightily through the community of Burgettstown through Mamma's witnessing, and we established a church. It was a Holy Spirit anointed place. We had revival every meeting. We thought that was not only proper, but a necessity. We founded our church on the Word of God, and our bylaws and our guidelines were taken from the Bible. When problems arose, we asked, "What saith the Word of God?" We found the answer to every problem in the Bible.

Each family sat in the church as a group, the children with their parents. There was no visiting, no talking. We carried a bit of the Catholic tradition with us, for we would kneel, pray, and sit down. Our pastor, Louis Montecalvo, a shoe repairman from Washington, Pennsylvania, received no salary. He was dedicated to the service of the Savior and King. He drove from Washington to Burgettstown, approximately thirty-six miles round trip, each Sunday and Wednesday and one other day, which he called "visitation day," when he visited the families of the church.

Pastor Montecalvo was one of the older boys of the Montecalvo family who called at our farmhouse that eventful Sunday afternoon when Mamma was saved and filled with the Holy Spirit. In addition to taking care of his pastorate, he traveled from Washington to the area communities, picked up shoes and other footwear at various collection depots and took them back to his shoe shop to make the necessary repairs.

The pastor gave the some 200 church members a two-week advance notice of the observance of the Lord's Supper. He told us to prepare ourselves. "If you have said anything about anyone, get it straightened out. If you have aught against anybody, make it right. If you have any hate in your heart, get it out." He insisted upon spiritual preparedness for Holy Communion. He demanded strict adherence to the Word of God.

Things began to happen when the two-weeks' notice to prepare for Holy Communion was given. Some brethren traveled many, many miles to visit others toward whom they had ill feelings. They would embrace, ask forgiveness, and God blessed. But there were some who held out until the last minute. Then, during the singing and blessed choruses of praises to God on the day of Communion, a sister would get up on one side of the church and another on the other side, and they came rushing toward one another, meeting in the middle aisle. There they embraced each other, cried over their misdeeds, and asked each other's forgiveness. Any who failed to meet the forgiveness requirements were forbidden to participate in the Lord's Supper. They sat in their pews, weeping and trying to pray themselves through their problems.

At the Communion table, we all drank out of one cup. It was amazing that no one ever contracted any sickness or disease, but God takes care of such matters in His own way.

We believed and relied upon God and ran our church the biblical way. God blessed us with a constant revival. Anyone who came sick and desired healing was healed. Any seeking infillment with the Holy Spirit, if they were sincere in their hearts, got the baptism. Despite our walking in as close a harmony with God as we knew how, our church suffered persecution. The townspeople were predominantly Roman Catholic, and they were not tolerant of a small group of people going from door to door, telling the inhabitants about Jesus.

Italians comprised about 75 percent of the town's population and some of the fiery-tempered husbands became enraged when their wives were saved and filled with the Holy Spirit, and then they brought their children into the new church. Many women were terribly beaten and abused, but they continued to attend our Pentecostal church.

My godmother became a member and faithful supporter of our church, but my godfather just couldn't buy this "Holy Roller" religion. The man loved me with all his heart. He bought me my first pair of shoes, my first pair of long trousers. But things changed after I became a Pentecostal.

I met him one day on the street while on my way to church. He stopped me and, with tears in his eyes, said, "I no longer am your godfather." He reached in his pocket, took out his wallet and from it snatched a picture I had given him of myself when I was in the first grade in grammar school. He thrust the picture into my hand, saying, "I never want to see you again."

He stood six feet tall and was about 190 pounds of bone and muscle, a very rough, tough individual. His wife measured barely above five feet. Every time she attempted to come to our church, he beat her. One Sunday in particular she started to leave the house.

"You're not going to that church!" he bellowed.

"Oh, yes, I am."

"All right! I'll take care of you."

He grabbed her little New Testament and then gathered the few dresses she had in a clothes closet and threw them in a potbellied stove in the living room. He slammed the door shut, opened the bottom draft door, and the fire began to blaze. She left for church in her bedroom slippers and a cotton dress. He stood in front of the stove until it became red hot. Then, he soliloquized, "We'll see what kind of God you serve."

After a few minutes, he opened the door and looked into the fire. Suddenly he turned as gray as ashes. The dresses had burned, but in the center of the licking flames lay the little New Testament book, not even singed. He dropped the poker, reached both hands into the flames, grabbed the New Testament, pulled it out of the fire, and with burned hands, held it caressingly against his chest.

He ran to the woodshed and hid the New Testament in the rafters. Daily he visited that shed, opened the Bible and read it. One Sunday he decided he would sneak into the Pentecostal church while worship services were in progress. He entered through the back door and went into the basement, where he stood listening to the services in the sanctuary above.

That very Sunday, I happened to go to the basement on an errand and saw my godfather hiding behind the furnace. I ran back upstairs, two steps at a time, rushed to the pulpit and told the pastor, "Brother Boni, my godfather, is downstairs behind the furnace."

Praise God! The pastor whispered to the saints of God that Brother Boni was down below, and they prayed, praised God, and shouted exaltations as they never had done before. They prayed down conviction. They prayed down salvation. They prayed down deliverance. The power of God, in answer to the prayers, began giving that man behind the furnace a rough time. I don't know how he managed to remain in the basement, but God was not through with him. During the week he came to me and confessed how he had burned his wife's dresses and tried to burn the New Testament but it withstood the fire as did the three men in the fiery furnace of the Old Testament in the Book of Daniel.

The following Sunday, Brother Boni came to church again. This time he came through the front door. He went to the altar, knelt down and prayed and wept through to full salvation, was saved and filled with the Holy Spirit. God had moved greatly on this man, and that is the kind of God we serve.

Brother Boni and his wife had attended that first prayer meeting Mamma held in our home. They were but one of many couples started on the road to salvation and baptism in the Holy Spirit at that initial prayer meeting. Mamma continued those meetings each week on Monday night. If you want your church to grow, if you want your church to be strong, have prayer meetings. They will become the backbone of your church if they are God-centered prayer meetings.

At one of Mamma's meetings, a Russian family was saved and filled with the Holy Spirit. The man stood six-feet-four and weighed almost 240 pounds. He accepted Jesus Christ with open arms, as did the other members of his family. He was so excited with his newfound salvation that he wanted Mamma to hold a prayer meeting in his home. One Sunday afternoon, Mamma and some members of the church went to his home.

The family lived in an area of Burgettstown called Dago Hill. No one quite understood how he happened to move his family there, for it was the only non-Italian family in the whole area. I went with Mamma and her friends, and we filled his house so full that it seemed we were about to be crowded out either through the windows or up through the roof rafters. We witnessed, we sang, and we praised God and prayed. It must have been around eight o'clock in the evening when we all were down on our knees, singing, "Oh, Lord, send the fire. Send the fire! Send the fire!"

All the windows were open, and our singing probably

could be heard for blocks. Undoubtedly this was the reason why the repetition of the word, "Send the fire! Oh, Lord, send the fire!" brought such a quick response, but not from the authority we had expected. Suddenly we heard fire truck and police car sirens outside. The next instant, the fire chief was rushing to the front door, dragging a fire hose in one hand and carrying an ax in the other. The Russian brother got up off his knees and went to the door.

"Where's the fire?" shouted the fire chief.

"There's no fire here," said the Russian. "We got a prayer meeting here."

"Well, one of your neighbors called in and said you were shouting, 'Fire! Fire!' "

"You can't put this fire out."

The fire chief turned to his men. "There's no fire here. It's a prayer meeting."

Many unusual situations and healing miracles were experienced in Mamma's ministry. She learned to meet each situation with the blessed assurance that God was with her and in command. She believed in Rom. 8:31: "If God be for us, who can be against us?" and Matt. 17:20: "If ye have faith . . . nothing shall be impossible unto you."

One evening her faith was severely tested. She was asked to pray for a demon-possessed woman of the church who had tried to receive the baptism in the Holy Spirit. She was so filled with demons that the baptism was impossible. Mamma decided the situation had to be confronted. She and our pastor and a dynamic woman of God from Pittsburgh decided to lock themselves in the church and fast and pray over this demon-possessed woman until she was delivered. Another woman insisted upon joining the prayer group, but the Holy Spirit witnessed to Mamma and told her this woman should not take any part in the exorcism of the demons because she was not yet ready to enter into this type of gift from the Holy Spirit. The woman insisted. The pastor and others acquiesced, took her into the church with them, and began to pray for the possessed sister. As they prayed, the afflicted woman put her head between her knees, rolled herself into a ball and began to bark like a dog and foam at the mouth. The demons attacked her from every direction. The devil tried to distract Mamma, the pastor, and the two sisters.

There were 200 chairs in this particular room of the church, 100 on one side and 100 on the other, with the aisle separating them. All the chairs moved from side to side and went back again into the exact spot where they were initially. Not one chair was out of order. The moving of the chairs was a distracting device used by the devil, but Mamma and her prayer warriors continued to plead the blood of Jesus Christ and seek God.

They laid hands upon the demon-possessed woman as she lay on the floor, rolled up in a ball. The sister who pleaded to come along also laid hands upon the woman. She had her fingers interlaced, and the instant she touched the demoniac she began saying, "Come out of her! Come out of her!" Suddenly Satan bound her also. She could not pull her hands apart. She screamed and rolled over on the floor, her hands locked together by the interlaced fingers. It reminds me of Acts 19:15: "Jesus I know, and Paul I know; but who are ye?"

Mamma, the sister from Pittsburgh, and the pastor had to turn their attention from the other woman and lay hands on the recently possessed one. They prayed over her, and she was delivered. To protect her from any further demons, Mamma asked her to leave, that they might give their complete attention to the other sister without further interference by the demonic spirits.

They prayed for hours over the demon-possessed woman, and then suddenly the power of God encompassed the room. The whole church began to vibrate with the holy presence of God. The sister was set completely free. Praise God for steadfastness, and praise Him for people who dare to believe in

Him!

Mamma was always witnessing during my years of grammar and high school. I would take her to a town early in the morning in my high-school years and leave her to witness. Then, when I was out of school in the late afternoon, I would drive my car to the town and bring her home. Her feet and ankles would be severely swollen and painful, but the joy of the Lord was in her heart.

We were attending a little church in Weirton, West Virginia. People were being saved and filled with the Holy Spirit in great numbers. The pastor, for some undisclosed reason, quit and left the area. We took over stewardship of the church. Services sometimes would continue through the evening until one-thirty the next morning.

One cold winter morning we came out of the service at one-thirty. Mamma and my sisters, Jessie and Dolly, got into the car for the seventeen-mile-drive to Burgettstown. I slid behind the wheel, turned on the ignition, and stepped on the starter. The motor never even coughed. I switched on the dashboard lights.

"Oh, no!" I exclaimed. "Our gas tank is empty."

"Don't worry," Mamma said. "You just go ahead. Hey God! You bless this car. You make it take us home."

This was a real test of faith. I had to see this one. An empty gas tank! I mean that needle was plumb against the empty peg. It made no difference to Mamma. Her God was her source of supply.

"Frank! You try the motor again."

I stepped on the starter. The motor coughed, sputtered, and started. It skipped a few times while warming up, and I thought it was going to quit. But it didn't. I drove five miles and then ten miles, and Mamma was praying, "Hey God! See, God! You make the car take us home."

Mamma put a little more emphasis in her talking to God if the car gave a little jerk or coughed as though the engine was about to quit. We arrived in front of our house and the motor died. It merely quit and would not start again. We had traveled seventeen miles on an empty gas tank. That's mileage. It was the faith of Mamma. Glory to God!

During those high-school years I met in my school a beautiful girl, Julia Cujas, who wasn't saved, so was not infilled with the Holy Spirit. Neither she nor her family attended Mass regularly, although they were Roman Catholics of French descent. I fell desperately in love with her. She was a straight-A student, but she did not participate in any extracurricular activities of the school. She was beautiful, wholesome, and to me the most wonderful person in the world. After our high-school years we kept in contact.

On Easter Sunday, 1942, I asked Julie to come home with me and meet my family. She was an immediate hit. But I wasn't quite ready to chalk up the day and occasion as a success. There was Mamma, and Mamma could very sweetly learn about one's relationship with Jesus Christ.

"What church you go to, Julie? You have asked Jesus to come into your heart?"

It all came out; Julia was a Roman Catholic who did not attend Mass regularly. But worse in Mamma's thinking, she was not saved and filled with the Holy Spirit. Mamma did not mention the baptism in the Holy Spirit to Julie, and I was so glad because she would not have known what it meant, and I would have had to explain it to her later. I didn't want to do that for fear I might lose her. Mamma was sweet to her while she was in our home, but the next day she zeroed in on me. Both she and our pastor said I just could not become associated with any girl who was not compatible with Pentecostalism.

They might have made a deeper impression on the four winds by casting their objections upon them. I was so deeply in love with that girl that I would not heed anyone's advice. She was for me and I knew it. I would have it no other way. I meant to marry her—and soon—because our country was at war, and any day I might be taken into a branch of the armed forces. I wanted our marriage to come ahead of that. And so did Julie.

We saw each other frequently during the next few months. Then, on November 11, 1942, I asked our pastor to marry us and he refused. Mamma objected vehemently to our marriage. I insisted just as vigorously, and finally our pastor consented to perform the ceremony, saying, "I'll marry you under protest." He added, "Frank, I just wish you would get her prayed through and filled with the Holy Spirit."

I still was scared to tell Julie about the baptism in the Holy Spirit for fear of losing her. Sometimes we build mountains of fear which are little more than papier-mâche when put to the acid test. Even worse, Mamma and I both had failed, for once, to place our problem in the Lord's hands. How wrong we were proved to be.

Julie and I were married, and not too long afterward I was drafted into the Army and stationed at Fort Riley, Kansas. I sent for Julie. She joined me, and we stayed at the guesthouse in the Army camp. Every night Julie would pray on one side of the bed, and I prayed on the other side. We each prayed in our own way.

One night, after we had finished with our prayers and gotten into bed, she said, "Honey, I would like to pray."

"But we just got through praying," I said.

"Honey, I have got to pray. I can't tell you why, but I know we must pray NOW."

We slipped out of bed. This time I knelt down beside her, and we held hands. The minute our knees touched the floor, the power of God saturated our bodies. Julie was saved and filled with the Holy Spirit. She began speaking in tongues. It was glorious. God was so wonderful. Julie and I both were in the Spirit, and we had the same vision.

We no longer were in that little room in the guesthouse at Fort Riley. We had been transferred to a big, beautiful field of wheat. We could see the golden-bearded heads of wheat atop the stalks swaying in the breeze. We were clad in beautiful white robes, and we exalted and glorified our Lord.

God is always the giver of good things, if we will only believe and receive. He didn't let us realize for one single moment that we were in that little room in the guesthouse, because such a realization might have quenched the Holy Spirit. We were free to glorify the name of God.

The next day I could hardly wait to get to the telephone to call Mamma and tell her that Julie had received the baptism in the Holy Spirit. When finally I got her on the line, I said, "Mom, Julie—"

"Yes," she said. "Julie has got the baptism in the Holy Spirit."

I learned that that very night Mamma had been on her knees at ten o'clock, telling God, "Hey God! Give my son a saved wife."

God heard her prayer and sent His Holy Spirit upon Julie to convict her that night after we had finished our prayers and gotten into bed. She was so impelled to go back to prayer again that she could not resist the power leading her. Mamma's prayers were getting through to God as they always seemed to do, and God was moving in His mighty and wondrous way. Glory be to God!

Mamma had her heartaches despite her closeness to God. Six of her seven sons were in the armed forces during World War II. Joe, my oldest brother, was not accepted for service because of an injury he suffered as a child. Tony was a member of the 101st Airborne, a paratrooper. He was captured and killed during the Allied invasion of Europe. Costy died from service-connected injuries. Carmen, fighting with the Allies in Germany, served in the Third Armored Division. He was hit ten times by machine-gun fire, was hospitalized in England, and spent a long recuperative period.

The war was tragic for Mamma, but she went on thanking the Lord, thanking God for the children who were saved. She was not bitter or angry in any way but thanking the Lord continually for all things and remembering the latter part of Job 1:21: "The Lord gave, and the Lord hath taken away; blessed be the name of the Lord."

I was mustered out of the Army and returned to Burgettstown where Mamma still was holding her weekly Monday-evening prayer meetings. At almost every meeting we saw tremendous miracles as God moved mightily in our midst. People were saved, baptized in the Holy Spirit, and healed. I looked upon miracles which would astound anyone but those who actually believed Eph. 3:20: "Now unto him that is able to do exceeding abundantly above all that we ask or think, according to the power that worketh in us."

One evening a Sister Reed came to our prayer meeting and announced that she had undergone some medical tests in a hospital which showed she was full of cancer. The doctors said there was no hope for her. God knew differently. We laid hands on her and prayed, and the power of God came down on that humble little Sister Reed. She began to dance in the Spirit and to glorify and praise Jesus. A few weeks later she returned to the hospital for another physical examination. No trace of cancer was found. She still is praising and glorifying God. At our prayer meetings, praying for a cancer cure was no different than praying for the cure of a common cold.

We experienced miracles other than healing. This particular one happened after we had moved from the farm back to Burgettstown and directly in the midst of a Catholic neighborhood. Mamma continued to hold her prayer meetings. She would open the windows, and you could hear us singing four blocks away. An alley ran alongside our house, and one Monday evening, while we were holding a prayer meeting, nearly three dozen people came marching down the alley, led by their priest. I don't know what they intended doing, but they came and stood outside the house, and looked through the windows to where we were praying in the living room, which was next to a big sun porch.

It was a beautiful clear night. The stars were twinkling

from their heavenly berths, and a bright moon lighted the sky. It was a calm night, too, except inside where we were praying, shouting, and speaking in tongues. Suddenly a mighty rushing wind came through the trees and up over the rooftop. Seconds later came a mighty clap of thunder, followed by one of the worst electrical storms I have ever witnessed. The lightning flashed, and the thunder crashed and resounded through that alley and all around our house.

It was no night to be on the outside looking in, and our visitors realized it. Probably Mamma was the first to understand the situation. She went to the door and invited the visitors to come inside. It didn't take a second invitation. At least thirty, possibly half a dozen more, Catholics crowded into our sun porch and soon were on their knees with their rosaries. We had the biggest group in our prayer meeting history. Many of the newcomers became our friends and not only came to our prayer meetings but joined our church. We learned later that they had come to heckle us. That first clap of thunder had sent the priest running back to his church and left the parishioners to make their own decisions. Truly, God works in mysterious ways His wonders to perform.

One Monday evening after the Foglio family had moved to Fontana, California, Mamma received a telephone call from Sister Sarracino back in Burgettstown. Weeping as she talked over the telephone, she said, "Sister Foglio, I am sick. I had been feeling weak, and I went to the doctor. He gave me some tests and said I was full of sugar. I have diabetes. He said I had had the disease for years and didn't know it. There is no hope."

Mamma told her not to worry about it. At prayer meeting that night, we took a clean handkerchief, laid hands on it, and Mamma prayed: "Hey God! Bless this handkerchief. God, anoint this handkerchief. And God, when she puts it on her body, let her be healed. In the name of Jesus, Amen."

We mailed the handkerchief to Sister Sarracino, and a short time later we received another telephone call from her.

She had just returned from her doctor's office where not one trace of sugar was found in her blood. The doctors could not understand it. She could. We could. Glory be to God! Hallelujah! Such tremendous faith! "For I am the Lord that healeth thee" (Exod. 15:26).

Mamma had carried on many years of rewarding work for the Lord by the time we moved to Fontana. Only heaven will record the souls she won. Every time she won a family to the Lord, that family would win a family, and so it went through the years as she carried out her door-to-door witnessing campaign in six towns. She witnessed to everyone, including Dad. He had his chance, and what happened to him, and the way it came about, was quite unusual.

Cook the Spaghett

Cook the Spaghett

While Mamma progressed in her work for her Lord under the anointing of the Holy Spirit, she grew sweeter and sweeter. But Dad, on the contrary, seemed adversely affected by Mamma's service for the Lord. His cantankerous disposition grew worse and worse.

Most of Dad's close acquaintances called him Little Jim. He came in a small package, but what a stick of dynamite. When he gave us an order, we didn't question him. He told us to do something just once, and if we didn't do it, we'd get the worst whipping you can imagine. If he said, "Frank, you dig a hole here," I dug the hole. I wouldn't dare ask why. If he came back later, saw the hole was dug and said, "Fill it!" I'd fill it. We were all the same when it came to Dad. He said do it, and we jumped to get it done.

He kept us busy six days a week. On Sunday we would go out and sit under the apple trees on our farm. But those other six days of the week, each one of us children was assigned certain duties. Odd as it may seem, he had an unusual method: psychology. He could neither read nor write, but he was the smartest man, in some respects, I ever met. I discovered that much later in life.

Psychology! Dad could teach a psychologist. He would get mother up early in the morning, before he went to work at the roundhouse on the railroad, and outline the work of the day for each one of us. When he returned home in the evening, he wouldn't ask Mamma, "Did Frank do his work?" No! He had Mamma trained. He would sit down, and she would read the report to him. Right down the line she went. If I hadn't taken care of my chores, she would hold out my name until last and end with, "Frank went and played with the neighborhood boys."

Do you think Dad would react, "Hey! You little brat! Get over here"? No. He would pretend that he hadn't heard Mamma or, at least, he would act as though he hadn't. But when I walked by him, he would look at me with eyes like pieces of burning coal. At the table he would watch me out of the corner of his eye.

Dad was the kind of man that, if we had company, wouldn't say, "Frank! George! You leave the room." He would look at us with eyes that literally picked us up out of our chairs as a magnet might draw a piece of iron. Nowadays, to get your children out of the room you have to give them a couple of judo clips and drag them out by the heels. Chances are they will crawl back in again. No respect.

You didn't fool with my dad. He'd look up at me and say, "I don't care if you are taller than I am and weigh more. As long as you're under my roof, I'm the boss. See?" He meant it. You didn't con him, or threaten him. We didn't dare try it, not even after we were full-grown and each one of us made two of him.

He had his system. When you didn't do your job, he would let one day, two days, sometimes three days go by before he dealt out the punishment. All this time you'd be sweating it out, and he could make you sweat. He didn't care what you did. The punishment waited usually until you were practically a nervous wreck. Then some early morning you would hear him coming up the stairs. You knew this was it. You would roll over on your belly before he got into the room. He wouldn't say a word. He wouldn't tell you that you didn't do your job. Nothing.

One morning I pulled a fast one. I traded places with my brother George. I should have stayed where I was. He whipped George with a belt. He knew where to lay it on. And all during the whipping, George was shouting, "Dad! Dad! It's me, George!"

"So it makes no difference," Dad said after he had finished. "Maybe next week you do something wrong. So, you already got your beating."

George took care of me afterward. I never traded places with him again. You just couldn't win with Dad. He was the boss, and he made certain everyone knew it. There were no exceptions, not even Mamma. That was the kind of home we had, and that was the way we were disciplined. One family! One head!

Somewhere along the line, Dad developed the habit of bringing some of the work crew home with him from the railroad roundhouse after a day's work. The roundhouse was four miles from home. One afternoon he walked into the house with two engineers and two firemen. He looked at Mamma and said, "Cook the spaghett." That's all he said. He didn't ask if she had spaghetti or if there was enough for all of them. "Cook the spaghett." Mamma knew she had better cook the spaghett and ask no questions.

We were plenty short on modern conveniences of the times, but we ate well. Dad never asked where the food came from, how much it stretched the purse strings, or how low in supplies the cupboard might be. He liked to eat. He ate well and usually told Mamma what to cook. He was a generous man when it came to food. No one ever left our home hungry; in fact, he would invite strangers to sit down to a meal, even though they were only passing by, if he thought they appeared to need food.

One day a black man came by and Dad stopped him. "You hungry?" he asked. The stranger said he was. "Come in and eat." The man came inside and Dad handed him a plate of spaghetti. The man walked outside, sat down on the porch steps and began to eat. That really pushed up Dad's blood pressure.

"Hey, you!" he shouted, rushing out onto the porch. "Do

you think you are so much better than we are that yuh can't come in and eat with us? Come in here and sit with us." The man came in and Dad converted him—Slim Hopper—to the Italian Club.

We bought spaghetti by the twenty-pound box and kept it in the cupboard. Mamma went to the cupboard on this particular night that Dad brought the two engineers and two firemen home. She took out the spaghetti box and looked in it. There was less than a quarter of a pound of spaghetti. Not nearly enough. The closest store was five miles away. We had no means of transportation except by mare's shank. We had no telephone, no indoor plumbing, and no electric lights. Our only lighting system was kerosene lamps.

I watched Mamma. She took the spaghetti and didn't blink an eye as she laid it on the table. Then she ran like a scared cat into the living room and returned with that little black book. She grabbed the spaghetti from the table, held it above her head in one hand and raised the New Testament above her head in the other hand.

"Hey, God!" she said, "I have to say please. Hey! Look, God! I read it today. How you feed the multitude with five loaves and two fishes. See? You just the same today. You no change. Huh!" She asked God to bless the spaghetti, and then she began to make those funny noises. Usually this would send the rest of the family rushing off to pretended other chores. But I stayed. I wanted to see what would happen.

She set the spaghetti on the table along with the sauce. Then she went to the cupboard, got the biggest platter and the biggest pot she could find, and set them on the table. She filled the pot with water and put it on the coal stove. Finally, she had everything underway, and stood with the little black book in one hand, stirring everything on the stove with a wooden spoon she held in the other hand.

The water started boiling in the big pot. Mamma took the spaghetti, and I watched her put it into that boiling water. It went "shoooost!" and was lost, about like putting a drop of sea water into a spoon. She stirred and stirred, and when the spaghetti was fully cooked, she started serving it. She bailed it out and bailed it out. I couldn't believe what I was seeing as Mamma stood there bailing out that spaghetti. I thought, "Will she never stop?" She filled the platter to overflowing. She didn't blink an eye. No surprise, shock, or fainting. It was supposed to happen.

"You can't lie God. Hey! Hey!"

She called the family: twelve Foglios, two engineers, two firemen, and two neighbor's kids. Eighteen sat down at our big dinner table. Each one ate all he could hold. The next day, twelve Foglios ate the leftovers and had plenty to eat—all from less than a quarter of a pound of spaghetti. God still keeps His Word. Don't let anyone tell you miracles don't happen anymore!

Isn't it about time we wise up? We put out our fleeces. We fast. We ask everyone to pray, and we pray about the same things day and night. But do we actually commit it to God? Think about it! A little woman and a quarter of a pound of spaghetti. She used what she had in her hand. She held it up to God. "Here it is, God. It's all I have. Bless it! It's all Yours. You're the same God who fed the multitude with five loaves and two fishes. You're the same today. You will not fail in Your promises."

Yes! Mamma said, "It's all Yours. Bless it!" And He did. She let go and let God do it.

I don't suppose Mamma ever told Dad about how God blessed and multiplied the spaghetti that night. The situation had changed in our home. Whereas Mamma used to be scared of Dad, now it was the reverse. Dad wasn't really scared of *her*. He just didn't want to take any chances on what might happen to him if he wrongfully and willfully struck the anointed one. He stayed away from her. He didn't talk to her. But his disposition and his meanness grew worse. Then one day something happened.

Dad was sitting in the kitchen with his wine and his pipe.

Mamma wasn't critical of people who had habits. She didn't look at anyone's habits. She was more concerned with their souls. She didn't look at the cigarette or the pipe or the alcoholic breath. She wanted only to bring the soul to Jesus, and once that was accomplished, everything would fall into line in due time. She never criticized Dad. He would curse us while we were praying, and she'd just smile and treat him with kindness.

This particular day while he was sitting in the kitchen with his pipe and wine, he began to cry. I had never seen him cry in my life. But now he was crying as though his heart was breaking. Suddenly he left his pipe and wine and ran into the living room where Mamma was ironing some clothes. The only irons she had were those old, cold irons that were heated on the stove—wedge-shaped and black with a handle.

"Mamma, I'm sick."

"What's wrong?" She didn't look up from the ironing board.

"I feel like I don't belong to this family anymore. I feel I'm lost. I'm separated. What am I gonna do?"

Mamma didn't say, "You're a dirty sinner. You've got to quit drinking wine, quit smoking your pipe." No! She continued ironing and didn't even give him a quick glance.

"You know what you gotta do. Do it!"

Dad fell on his knees, his fingers on the ironing board to steady himself. Mamma prayed. He prayed. They prayed together, and he was filled with the Holy Spirit. He was saved.

Accepting Jesus Christ as his Lord and Savior changed Dad instantly. What a witness he became for Jesus! But there were some trials and tribulations. He was reluctant to tell his friends and associates on the railroad that he had been saved and baptized in the Holy Spirit.

He continued to act rough away from home, although he did quit swearing, drinking, and smoking. He was delivered of all these habits. It was difficult for his railroad cronies to understand why Dad no longer participated in their habits when he gave no excuse for quitting.

One day one of the engineers said to Dad, "Little Jimmy, my wife had a baby boy yesterday." He handed Dad a cigar. Dad didn't say, "Well, I don't smoke anymore." He took the cigar and put it in his shirt pocket. Busy with his work, he soon forgot about the cigar. But Satan wasn't about to let him off the hook that easily. He reminded Dad that he had a very expensive cigar in his pocket. Old Satan knew where to hit and hit hard; Dad always had loved a good cigar.

Satan suggested that Dad just take the cigar out of his pocket. He didn't have to smoke it. He could merely take a good long smell of the sweet aroma. Dad took the cigar out of his pocket and tried to sniff it, but there was no aroma. Satan knew that. He said, "You can't smell anything through that wrapper. Take the wrapper off, and get a real whiff of that expensive cigar." Dad did as Satan suggested, and oh my, that cigar smelled so good, so tempting. He said later, "In all my life I never smelled anything that smelled so good. It smelled like a bouquet of roses."

Satan said, "You don't have to light it. You don't have to smoke it. Just take the end of it and roll it around in your mouth." Dad was a bit reluctant. He wasn't quite certain that he wanted to permit temptation to lead him that far. But Satan convinced him there was no harm, no sin, in just rolling the end of the cigar around in his mouth. Dad put the end of the cigar in his mouth and rolled it around.

"Oh, that tastes like milk and honey," he told himself.

Satan left him then. Dad returned the cigar to his shirt pocket and forgot about it until he arrived home that evening. Then he went into the barn to do a little work, and Satan came at him again, reminding him of that sweet-smelling cigar in his pocket. He said, "Why don't you just roll it around in your mouth again? You know how good the flavor was. It's not wrong. It's not a sin. You don't have to light it."

The temptation was too overpowering. Dad put the cigar

in his mouth, and Satan threw the haymaker. "Why don't you light it? You don't have to inhale. Just take a couple of puffs and then throw it away."

Again Dad followed Satan's suggestion. He took about three puffs and decided he had never tasted anything better in his life. "Oh," he told himself. "It tastes so good. It tastes better than a plate of spaghett."

In the midst of his ecstasy, Dad saw a beautiful, big white hand. It came through the air and slapped him across the mouth, cigar and all. The hand slapped Dad so hard that it knocked him against the side of the barn and cut his lip. Dad crushed the cigar under his heel and ran into the house, where he fell at Mamma's feet. He was weeping and shaking. Mamma asked, "What's the matter? What's the matter?"

"God hit me!"

"He must have had a reason. What you do wrong?"

"The devil! He tell me to smoke a big cigar. I seé a big hand. It hit me in the mouth."

"You deserved it. You shouldn't have smoked a cigar."

"Please, Mamma, pray for me?"

Mamma laid hands on him. She said, "Hey God! You bless him good. You console him. You make him smoke no more. Thank You, God."

When Dad started telling you about Jesus, you had to listen. He was a powerful man, despite his small stature. He would take by the hand a person to whom he wanted to witness. "I wanna tell you about Jesus." He learned this from Mamma.

It wasn't easy to pull your hand away from his firm grasp. You would listen, and after he finished witnessing, he would straighten your tie and show you a nice smile. He lived strong in the Lord, loyal and faithful to his death, which came a few years after the family moved to Fontana.

The day Dad went to be with the Lord, we thought surely there would be no prayer meeting that night. But we went into the living room and sat in our chairs and we waited. Soon Mamma came out of the bedroom. Tears were flowing down her cheeks, but she brushed them aside and made a pronouncement.

"Children, we gonna have a prayer meeting tonight. Daddy! He's not there in the funeral home. He's with Jesus."

We proceeded to have a sweet prayer meeting. Mamma prayed, "Hey God! You bless my kids. You console their hearts. You let them know that some day they're going to see Daddy. Thank You, God. Amen!"

Dad left me with a great many memories, some bad and some good. The best ones revolved around the later years of his life. I suppose I talked too much to suit him. I did and still do enjoy talking. But one day Dad said to me, "Son, you talk too much." Then he added, "He who think by the inch, and talk by the mile, ought to be kicked by the foot."

The advice didn't seem so important when Dad told me, but had I heeded those words, they might have spared me much trouble a few years later.

Don't Leave God Out

Don't Leave God Out

Some forty years ago I received the infilling of the Holy Spirit, and it is just as exciting today as it was then, perhaps more so. I feel the same tremendous power upon me. I begin to vibrate within me when I speak to others about the goodness of God. When I witness or give my testimony I feel the overflowing of the Holy Spirit throughout my body. Very often it's a prickling sensation that starts at the bottoms of my feet and runs up my legs, my back, down my arms into my hands and fingers, and back up again to the top of my head.

Can you imagine anyone losing that spine-tingling sensation once he has captured and experienced it? Can you imagine one so in harmony with God, losing that contact to the extent that he knows God has turned His back on him? That he no longer permits that intimate contact to exist? I lost that relationship.

God had blessed me abundantly with a wonderful Spirit-filled wife and two fine children. My position in the engineering department of Swift & Company supplied funds to meet our needs, although we lived on a payday to payday basis. I became afflicted with that age-old employee malady: overworked and underpaid. Discontentment can strike when things are going smoothly. That old devil, Satan, sneaks in and makes you believe you should be blessed more abundantly. Dissatisfaction! Self-pity! Impatience! These are tools of the devil, and I fell for them.

Something happened to me as I listened to the devil. I

began thinking I could do better with a business of my own. I became obsessed with this idea.

While my obsession grew, a most unusual development occurred. Clem Marone, his wife Mary Jo, and their two children moved to Fontana, and with them came Clem's father, Nick. Clem and his family were Roman Catholics, but Nick, a Spirit-filled man, wanted to associate with others of like faith and experience. Someone sent Nick to my mother, and Mamma told him about me.

Nick and Clem called on me one day with an idea that changed my life. Nick had a formula for making Italian sausage. He wanted my meat-processing experience and offered to set Clem and me up in business. There was no Italian sausage manufacturer in the area, and since Fontana and its environs had a large Italian population, I immediately envisioned building a large, successful business. I knew that my dream was on the road to reality as I walked into my home that evening after work and made a very simple but emphatic announcement.

"Honey," I said to Julie, "I'm never going to work for another man the rest of my life. I'm quitting now. I'll never wear these shoes again."

I took the shoes off my feet, put on bedroom slippers, and carried those old work shoes out into the garage. I never wanted to see them again. Returning to the living room, I reached that egotistical plateau crowned with the big "I."

"I'm going on my own," I told Julie. "I'm going to make big money, and I'm going to make it fast, regardless of anything or anyone. I mean it, Julie. I am determined. You know my nature. When I start to do something, I stay with it. I'm a very determined person."

Julie didn't say, "Have you consulted God? Have you talked to Him about it?" She said nothing. She knew and understood my attitude. Most wives understand their husbands much better than the husbands think they do. It would have been better for me had Julie reminded me of my dad's sage advice:

"He who think by the inch, and talk by the mile, ought to be kicked by the foot."

I do not wish to make any alibis for my departure from the Lord's ways, but I do think I was influenced by my oldest brother, Joe. He was an affluent businessman in Weirton, West Virginia. He had a beautiful home and drove big, expensive cars. He had a fat wallet and knew how to keep it fat. He was the epitome of affluence in his actions, dress, and behavior. Though he didn't know Jesus Christ, without the Lord he was doing very well.

I was going to become an affluent businessman, perhaps even more so than Joe. There was only one thing wrong. I was not taking the Lord into my plans. When you are out of contact with God, you can move swiftly into some terrible fates, and I was rushing headlong into one when, in January, 1955, I became a partner with the Marones in the Italian sausage producing company.

Clem Marone and his father, Nick, built the business around me. That was the first mistake. No business should be dependent upon a single individual for its operation. But I had meat-processing experience with Swift & Company, so my word was law. Clem, his dad, and I built a plant. We moved quickly. We became more and more involved in the construction of the plant and equipping it. Problems began to pop up. How did we meet them? Through human ingenuity. Not once did I consult God. Didn't even think about it. I was too busy.

I didn't ask, "God is this Your will? God, should I proceed in this direction?" I didn't seek God's face because I was afraid He would give me answers I did not want to hear. No! Frank Foglio was operating on his own ingenuity and cleverness. He was going to make big money and make it fast. Every morning I would be up with the telephone in one hand and a cup of coffee in the other. Time and time again during the day, God would try to deal with my heart. Mamma, I know, was praying for God to break through my pride and stubbornness. She was saying, "Hey God! My boy, Frank, You bless him."

I would hear God trying to answer Mamma's prayers, trying to speak to me, trying to break through my busy schedule. "Son! Son! Hearken unto Me!"

"God, I'm busy. Please wait. I'll talk to You tonight. God, honestly, I will talk to You tonight."

Night would come, and many other nights, but Frank Foglio was too busy to talk to God until bedtime. Then I would be so exhausted, I'd fall asleep on my knees, and my patient wife would wake me to get me to bed. I never did get into a conversation with the Lord; I was never an audience, because I was too exhausted or too busy to listen and talk to Him.

Never think you can turn God on and off as you would a cold- or hot-water tap. I learned that the hard way. I soon discovered that God was not going to let this Italian boy off so easily. God never forgets. He sets a plan, and He moves in mysterious ways to accomplish it. This I also learned the hard way.

During those tough, rough days I was in constant companionship with Clem Marone and his dad, Nick. Clem was a rough individual. He had been a former boxer and held three titles. During our business association, he showed no interest at all in Christianity or in learning about Jesus Christ. But his dad was an entirely different man.

Nick was five feet tall and five feet round. He didn't have a hair on his head or a tooth in his mouth, but he was full of the Holy Spirit. I didn't like him. Can you imagine that? My dislike was rooted in a habit he developed. We would be working in the plant, and Nick would come tiptoeing in. I wouldn't hear him. But I felt him. I knew he was in the building. Suddenly from behind me came a booming, *"Haaaa—leeee—luuuu—yaaah!"* It would come up from his arches. I'd feel the hair on the back of my neck stand right up, and I'd burst out with goose pimples all over my body.

Did you know that when you are out of the center of God's will, you cannot stand the praise of God's saints? I couldn't stand it. Every day he would make this little trip to wherever I might be working in the plant and let out with his bellowing, *"Haaaa—leeee—luuuu—yaaah!"* Why did he have to stand behind me to exercise his tonsils? He could have chosen any other place in the plant, any piece of equipment. No! Frank Foglio had to hear it.

One day I said to Clem, "Let's have a conference. Let's go into the office." I didn't want his dad to hear what I had to say.

"You know, Clem," I said. "Your dad is old. Suppose some day when he comes walking into this plant, the floor is slippery. What if he slips and falls and breaks his neck?" Under my breath I said, "I wish he would." Pretty hard talk for a man who once was under the baptism in the Holy Spirit.

Clem looked me straight in the eye. "Frank, you are forgetting something."

"What?"

"We're building, we're operating, and we're drawing our salaries on my dad's money."

I reached the plateau of my fate February 25, 1955. I am certain God would have decreed otherwise for me, had I allowed Him to break through my busyness to confer with me. But I hadn't even had time for my family. I was becoming a stranger in my own household. My Bible reading and prayers also had been sadly neglected. My business was all-important to me. Making money and making it fast was my goal.

Now I was ready to start reaping the harvest for which we had sowed so diligently and so indefatigably. February 25. The next day, the twenty-sixth, we would open the plant officially. Today we were testing the equipment to make certain all was in good operating order. What a wonderful feeling as I looked forward to that grand opening. We were so excited. We didn't hold a prayer meeting or have a thanksgiving service. We didn't need to thank God for the accomplishments. Thank God because everything was running so beautifully? Why? We had done it ourselves.

We began to test the equipment. We came to our meat-grinding machine which would grind 100 pounds of meat a minute. It worked beautifully. After we tested the grinder, Clem proceeded to clean it.

"Frank! Come quickly! Something's wrong!"

I hurried over to Clem and the meat-grinding machine. The knife that cuts the meat was missing. The wing nut was in place, but the knife was gone. Not a trace of it anywhere! It had just disappeared. Where? Where? We didn't understand it. That was the only knife we had. I should have had the foresight to buy an extra knife for an emergency. But I didn't.

"We'll have to drive into San Bernardino right away and buy another one," I said, and went home to get ready for the trip because I didn't want to make a business call in my work clothes.

A little later Clem and his dad drove up in front of my house in a brand-new pickup truck. They blew the horn. I went running out the door, as I always did when I was in a hurry. Once outside and in the yard, I felt something happen. I'll never forget that moment. A chill came over my body, just as if someone had dropped an ice-cold blanket over me. I shuddered for a moment.

Had I been in favor with God, as I should have been, I would have rushed into the house, fallen on my face, and asked God what that sudden chill meant. What should I do? I would have saved much sorrow and suffering. But, no! I started to walk down the driveway, strictly a piece of machinery, a man whose mind and heart and whole being were dedicated to promotion, to making money, big money, and making it in a hurry.

My little son came running to me and with outstretched

arms pleaded, "Daddy, take me? Take me with you, Daddy?"

He was such a good-looking, curly-headed little fellow and so sweet. I couldn't refuse him. I knew he would have to sit on my lap. I bent down to pick him up. I had my hands underneath his arms and started to lift him.

The voice of God said, "Don't do it!"

"Just a minute," I said, putting the boy down. Was that in my mind that I heard that voice? Was that actually God speaking to me? I started to pick up the little fellow again, and I heard the voice of Almighty God speaking to my heart and saying, "Don't do it!"

I looked at my wife and then to Clem and his dad, and I thought they had heard the voice, too. That did it. I backed away from my son. "I'll take you some other time," I explained and got into the pickup truck. We drove into San Bernardino and bought the knife for the meat-grinding machine.

We intended driving out of San Bernardino on the same route on which we came in, but a water main had broken, and we were detoured down San Bernardino Avenue. God sees ahead and He sets the scene. He wanted to detour this Foglio, slow him down to where he would have to listen to God speak, to get back into conversing with the Lord.

We were traveling about sixty-five miles an hour, in a hurry to return to the plant. Always in a hurry! At the intersection of Meridian and San Bernardino, an automobile collided with our vehicle. There were no stop signs on Meridian or San Bernardino. The driver of the car didn't see our truck, and Clem, driving the pickup truck, didn't see the car. The car, traveling sixty-five miles an hour, hit my side of the pickup truck. My body smashed against the windshield. The door was ripped off its hinges. I was thrown thirty-five feet. Still conscious while flying through the air, I remember saying, "This is it."

I had another thought, also. "God is merciful." My son would have been sitting on my lap had I taken him with us.

He would have died in my arms, crushed to death.

Both Clem and Nick were thrown out of the pickup and onto the highway. I landed on the back of my neck. When I regained consciousness, I was in Kaiser Hospital, looking up at the bright lights in the ceiling of the operating room. I was surprised to find that I was alive. I thought I had died at the intersection when the vehicles collided.

I began to take inventory. My right arm was strapped to my body. I couldn't move it. The sight in my right eye was dim, and I had severe pains in my head and throughout my body. All my teeth were chipped, and my mouth was full of sand. My left arm was bruised and bloody.

It's amazing that I didn't shout for my wife, Julie, or Clem or Nick. The first words I uttered were, "Oh, God!" I knew in my heart that I was out of the center of God's will. If He had taken me then, I would have been lost for all time and eternity. But I was alive.

I began to wonder about my partner and his dad. What had happened to them? I soon learned that Clem had suffered a split tailbone, been treated and sent home. But I could learn nothing about Nick.

The doctor and a male nurse moved me off the operating table and into a wheelchair. They wheeled me down a corridor with rooms on either side. The male nurse said, "Every ward is packed. I don't know where we will put him." Suddenly the nurse stopped pushing the wheelchair and headed it toward a room. "There's a bed in there," he said, after looking into the room. I was wheeled in and put into the only empty bed on the floor.

God always sets the scene. In the next bed I saw my partner's dad, Nick Marone. He was propped up with his head completely bandaged. There he was, in a hospital robe meant for someone six-feet-seven. It made him look like a fat, bruised baby. He lay there with his mouth gaping open.

"Shall I tend to him?" the male nurse asked the doctor, nodding in Nick's direction.

"No!" came the reply. "He's not going to live to see morning. The undertaker will take care of him."

Right then I realized I didn't want Nick Marone to die. I began to plead with God. "Oh, my God! No, God! No! No! You cannot let him die, God. You cannot take him. It wasn't his fault, God. Why should he suffer? It wasn't his fault. It's all my fault. I deserve to be the one to go. I deserve to be punished. Oh, God, why not leave him down here? He loves You."

I realized God was not hearing me for the first time in years. I had been so busy, so preoccupied, and so out of contact with God that I didn't realize God had turned His back and was not hearing me. He wasn't interested in a thing I had to say. He would do as He pleased. He didn't need me to tell Him what to do.

I was determined now to break through to God. "God, it's because I'm not in Your will that he's lying there, dying. God, please don't let him die. I know I was ashamed to speak Your name in public, God. I was ashamed to witness and testify. But now I'm not ashamed, God. Please don't take him home. It's my fault. Please heal him. God?"

The doctor and the nurse looked at me, shook their heads, and walked out of the room as the doctor said, "He's delirious." I continued to pray.

My words bounced off the ceiling and back into my face. I kept calling out to God, and after the midnight hour, a mighty bright light flashed into the room. It was like a thousand powerful light bulbs shining—supernatural prisms. I knew we had a visitor from heaven. A powerful force came into that room, shaking the bed, the entire room. I couldn't move. I couldn't shout. But I could observe everything.

The most beautiful hand extended between the two beds. Above the hand was a gorgeous, white, flowing sleeve. I recognized the hand of my Lord, the nail-scarred hand of Jesus. I heard the same voice that said to me, "Don't do it!" as clearly as when it had first spoken the afternoon I started to pick up my little son to take him with us in the pickup truck to San Bernardino. Now, that voice was speaking to me again.

"Fear not, for I will take care of him."

The hand moved forward, took hold of the bandages on Nick's head, and squeezed until the very blood oozed through the fingers of my Lord.

Then the hand pointed in my direction, and I fell into a deep sleep.

A Miraculous Healing

A Miraculous Healing

The next morning I was awakened by a young, pretty nurse. She was calling, "Nick! Nick! Nick!" I looked over, and Nick hadn't moved. He looked as dead as a person laid out in the morgue. I said, "Lord, what did You do? Lord, You were here last night. You said You would heal him. Now, You have taken him home. Why did You do it?"

The nurse continued saying, "Nick! Nick! Are you all right?"

Then she did something that scared both of us practically to death. She reached over and grabbed Nick by the arm and shook him. She shouted, "Nick! Are you all right?"

That little man leaped out of bed and hit the floor running, both hands high in the air, shouting, "Thanks be to God, I'm fine." He danced around and around, shouting and speaking in tongues. We had a revival right there, and it was Nick's. The nurse dashed out of the room and ran down the corridor, screaming, "He's alive! He's alive."

She found the doctor and dragged him into the room. I knew she must have dragged him, because I could see, as they stood in the doorway, that she had a half-hammerlock on him and was so excited she didn't really know what she was doing.

"Look! Look!" she shouted. "He's alive!" Nick was running around and around, his hands in the air, speaking in a heavenly language.

The doctor looked dumbfounded. He was the one who had pronounced the death sentence on Nick the night before. He stood there for a minute, disbelieving what he was seeing, as Nick continued cavorting about the room and making those funny noises.

"You get back in that bed!" the doctor ordered when he found his voice. Nick shouted, "Thanks be to God. I'm healed! I'm fine!"

"Hey, you!" the doctor shouted, trying to make himself heard above the noise made by Nick hopping and jumping about and praising the Lord.

"Hey, you! Get back in that bed!"

"Oh, no! No! I'm just fine. Jesus heal me last a night. Frank sick. Take care of him. I wanna go home."

I was crying and bawling and carrying on as Nick continued jumping and hopping about the room and speaking in tongues.

"Please get back in that bed?" the doctor pleaded.

"I get back in bed under one condition," Nick replied. "I keep Frank company."

The doctor agreed. Nick hopped into bed and began jumping up and down. The doctor approached him with the caution with which one would approach a rattlesnake. I didn't blame him. The doctor said, "Please! I want to check your heart." How do you listen to the heart of a man who is jumping and shouting and praising the Lord? He wanted to see if old Nick was still alive. Or was rigor mortis setting in?

The doctor said, "Please? Let me check something?" Nick became silent and sat quietly as the doctor reached up and slowly began to tear the bandages from Nick's head. He pulled them gently until he had removed every one, and as the bandages came off, the doctor's eyes grew bigger and bigger, first with disbelief and then with astonishment. He stepped back and took a long, quiet look at Nick's head.

"It's a miracle!" he exclaimed. "A miracle! He was next to dead yesterday, and now, not a mark. Not a stitch required. Every wound is clean and completely healed. A miracle!"

There was complete silence for almost a minute, then the

doctor shook his head. "I don't know what happened."

"I know what happened!" Nick shouted. "Jesus healed me last night. That's what happened!" Then he came forth from his arches with his *"Haaaa—leeee—luuuu—yaaah!"* It shook me, shook the room, and attracted the attention of everyone on the floor. They wanted to know what was going on in our room. Glory be to God! What a witness Nick's healing became! His doctor wanted to keep him in the hospital a few more days to make certain his healing was permanent. Nick agreed, only if he could keep me company. That was a mistake.

They brought in our breakfast. Nick didn't think I was worthy to pray for the food. He took over. He prayed for half an hour. He prayed for me that I might get spiritually fed. He didn't pray for my broken body. Then he spoke in tongues, and the eggs got cold. He could care less. I didn't eat my breakfast. He was humming, and singing, and speaking in tongues, and gumming his food all at the same time. And the way he was looking at my tray, I thought he was going to ask for my food, too. I was not able to feed myself, and as the food grew cold waiting for Nick to finish praying and praising the Lord, the nurse who was supposed to feed me left to attend to other duties.

The doctor returned. He said, "Foglio, we ran several X rays on you." I didn't know it. "I hate to tell you this," he continued. "You have a severe brain injury. You almost lost your right arm. Practically every disk in your spine is injured."

Every time the doctor explained an injury, Nick would say, "Thank You, God! Thank You, Jesus! Amen!" The doctor said, "The only thing that will help your arm is a major operation. We're going to put a hinge in and attach it to the lower bone and the shoulder bone." Nick shouted, "Thank You, Jesus!"

The doctor left, and old Nick grabbed his Bible. He began treating me as though I was one of the worst sinners that he had ever met. Holding his Bible, he said, "I'm gonna read some Script." He read five chapters and would have continued reading had not the male nurse come in to take me to the X-ray room for additional X rays.

When I returned, there was Nick propped up in bed with his Bible. He said, "We finish verse 35, chapter 38." That went on day and night. I heard more Scripture during the next few days than during any other period in my life. God had me where He wanted me, flat on my back where I couldn't get away from it. I had to hear, "For thus saith the Word of God," whether or not I liked it.

Despite Nick's Scripture reading and praising the Lord, things became worse for me. I suffered excruciating pain in my head and in every other part of my body. I also had a pain that no pill could kill, no injection could cure. It was with my soul. I could not reach God. I no longer had the comforting peace given by the presence of the Lord. I no longer experienced the joy of the Holy Spirit's power.

They moved me with blankets and X-rayed me day in, day out. I wasn't able to feed myself, to sit up, to turn my head. What dejection as I lay in that hospital bed, realizing only a few days ago I was a man strong in body, a man who loved to work, who enjoyed sports and loved to feel his muscles working. Now I was a helpless invalid, not knowing whether I would live from one day to the next.

I called out to God, pleading, "God, give it back to me!" He wouldn't even hear me.

The fifth day in the hospital, the doctor came into my room, walked up to my bed and said, "I've got good news for you. Your back is not broken. You have a brain concussion and a neck injury. Your spine is injured as I originally told you, and as you know, your right arm is seriously injured." He didn't say anything about surgery on the arm as he had the day after the accident.

The next day the male nurse came into the room. He said, "Mr. Foglio, your family is waiting to see you down the hall."

I'll never forget that day. I had a heavy growth of beard. I couldn't shave myself, and no one had shaved me. They put me in a wheelchair, and I felt like a man who had been resurrected from the dead, who had just come out of the grave; who had been given another opportunity to see what he had neglected. They wheeled me down the hallway, and it seemed my family was a thousand miles away. The wheelchair wasn't going fast enough.

I saw my son, my daughter, and my wife, and as I came closer, I realized I never had seen them look so beautiful. Julie and my daughter, Marilyn Joyce, were stunning beauties. I was ashamed to face them. I never thought I would see the day when I would be ashamed to face my family. But I was. When I did look up at them, they still looked so beautiful even at close range. They hadn't changed. They had always been that way. I just hadn't noticed.

I could almost hear God saying, "Here's another chance for you, Frank Foglio. You've come up from the grave. Here's a chance to observe what you've neglected. Not only have you neglected church, Sunday school, a prayer life, your family, and your God, but you have neglected My Word."

My little son, Frank Anthony, Jr., climbed up on the wheelchair and put his arms around me and hugged me. "I love you, Daddy." Right then I didn't care who heard me. I wrapped my good arm around him, almost in a protective manner, and I spoke to God from my very soul.

"Lord, he could have been dead. Lord, I could have been looking down into his casket. God, You spared me this grief. And God, You've given him back to me. God, he's Yours. You spared his life. I give him back to You. He's Your property, God. He's Yours." If ever I meant anything, this was it. And, for the first time, God heard me. I knew He heard me. I could not back down; it was no joking matter with God.

The next few days, following the visit by my family, were endless sessions of examinations and consultations. Because I refused to submit to surgery, it was decided there was nothing more that could be done for me at the hospital. They wanted to fuse my spine. I would never be able to bend over to tie my shoelaces or anything, once that was done. I would be like a robot walking on its heels. I would never be able to turn my head the remainder of my life. The doctors said my right arm might be helped somewhat, but I would never have complete use of it. Only time and God would heal my brain injury. The doctors said, "You are going to lie in a cast from your neck to your knees for nine months."

I said, "No! I will not!"

"Then you're on your own," was the final decision.

After my discharge from the hospital, I became religious. I wouldn't say super-religious, but I was looking for a healing of my body. Every evangelist who came to town found me in his prayer line, looking for God to touch my broken body. People in front of me were healed, and people behind me were healed, but I never received anything; however, God hadn't forgotten what I promised Him regarding my son.

Weeks after that promise, I was sitting in church with my family. Services had been dismissed, and members of the congregation were leaving. We had not moved from our pew. My son looked to the front of the church, pointed, and cried out, "I see Jesus! I see Jesus!"

The power of the Holy Spirit came down upon that congregation. Everyone in the church, in the doorway, and out in front were suddenly swaying in the Holy Spirit. The unsaved were saved, the backslidden came back, as we experienced a mighty moving of God. My son was filled with the Holy Spirit. He began speaking in tongues. He remained under the power of God for hours. He was the property of God, and God was doing a mighty work in his life.

I continued my quest for healing in prayer lines. I had so much anointing oil placed on my forehead that I felt it was going to run out of my shoes. Every preacher who prayed for the sick prayed for me, but nothing happened. One grabbed my bad arm and said, "Get it out of the sling." He took it out of the sling and twisted it, yanked it, and shouted, "In the name of Jesus!"

"Yes! In the name of Jesus, I'll be back in the hospital." My arm felt like he had torn all the ligaments loose.

It just wasn't my time. Regardless of who anointed me or prayed for me, it wasn't in God's will for me to be healed, because there was much fixing to be done in my life, a great deal of straightening out to be accomplished. Then, and only then, would God move on me.

One day I heard there was a prominent evangelist up in Bakersfield. He was conducting a big tent meeting. I thought sure if I could get to his meeting, and get in the prayer line, I would be healed. The most important immediate task was getting to Bakersfield. It was no simple matter for a man in my condition physically and financially.

I had kept in contact with Clem and Nick. After Nick left the hospital he held a forty-day fast for his son, praying that Clem would turn to Pentecostalism. Clem had married an Irish Catholic girl, Mary Jo, whom he had met in England, during the war. He was going to the Catholic church with her. One Wednesday evening shortly after Nick finished his fast, Clem called and said he would like to go to church with him. The pastor at the Assembly of God church preached the salvation message, and Clem received Jesus Christ into his heart. He was baptized with water, but did not receive the baptism in the Holy Spirit.

The following Sunday morning, Mary Jo asked Clem to get ready to go to confession with her and the two children. He replied that he did not need to confess his sins to any man. "I confessed them to the Lord in a water baptism at the Assembly of God church."

Mary Jo flew into a rage, grabbed Clem's shirt, and ripped it off his back. He smiled at her and said, "Praise God! Praise God!" Despite Mary Jo's violent protestations, Clem continued attending the Assembly of God church, and eventually there was a delightful turn of events which I will come back to later in the book.

The meat-processing business was actually staggering. Clem and Nick did not know how to operate it. They had depended entirely·upon me, and when you lean upon the arm of flesh you're in trouble. The business was so bad, they could no longer afford to pay me a salary. I had no finances. Mamma loaned me two dollars to go to Bakersfield.

Julie accompanied me on the drive to Bakersfield, where we found the Oral Roberts tent. I walked in, and even though I was in pain and slow of pace, I ignored all the little ushers, the flunkies, you know. Actually, nothing had happened to me inside—in my heart. I was broken in body, but still cocky. I was a smart aleck with many traits and habits that had to be put under the Blood; pride and a know-it-all attitude were but two of my faults. God had to deal with this Italian in His own way. That's why He was taking His time. He knew some adjustments had to be made in my life, and He had His own plan.

I made my way up to the head usher and said, "Sir!" I wasn't kind or considerate. "Sir! I have to get into the prayer line *tonight!*"

"Yeah! You and six hundred others." God knows how to answer a smart aleck.

"Sir! You don't know. I've got to get in *tonight!*"

"Fiddlesticks," he answered. "Why don't you get yourself a motel room and stay a couple of days. We'll be here."

I said to myself, "How come Oral Roberts engages this kind of an usher? This boy is not right." In my heart I knew the usher was right. He was experienced in handling smart alecks. I didn't even get a card for the prayer line. I thought the whole world was against me as I went back and sat down at the end of a row of seats.

It wasn't long before they started taking up the offering. The offering baskets were big ones. They looked like bushel baskets. I reached in my left coat pocket. Isn't it odd when it comes to an offering? We know where we've placed every one-dollar and five-dollar bill, and usually before the service we have separated the ones from the fives to make certain we're holding onto a one to put in the offering. Sometimes, by mistake, we put in the five and we panic. But I had only two ones, so I couldn't make a mistake. I separated them.

The bucket came in front of me, and I dropped a one-dollar bill in it. I heard the voice that said to me, "Don't do it!" when I was picking up my son to take him in the pickup truck into San Bernardino that fateful afternoon. It said to me, "You! Give two dollars!" I sat in the last chair in a row of seats, and the usher stood there, holding the bucket, paralyzed, but with a smile on his face. I said, "But, God!" The usher must have heard the voice of God, because he didn't move. He stood immobile, waiting for me to reach into my pocket and come out with that other one-dollar bill. I took a detour to get back into that pocket. I didn't want the usher to think he was going to get anymore out of me. I figured he would leave if I fiddled a little bit.   Stalled! But he remained standing there, a big smile on his face, until I went back into my pocket and came out with that other dollar bill—the last dollar I had—and dropped it into the bucket.

"Lord, now You've got it all," I said.

God doesn't like people to be thieves. I was a thief. I didn't believe in tithing. I thought if I gave ten dollars a month, that was good enough. Little did I know that I wasn't robbing God. I was robbing *me!* But today was different. This time the Lord had it all. "You've got it, God," I said.

I had no sooner uttered those words than Oral Roberts came onto the platform and began to tell us about his "Blessing Pact." He presented a delightful business proposition. He said, "If any of you can pledge one hundred dollars, I will put your name in my prayer book, and by the end of the year you will have gotten it back and more. If not, write me and I will return it."

I thought, "Yeah! That means everyone else but me. I don't have a hundred dollars, will never see a hundred dollars. So, why should I pledge that much money?" Oral seemed to read my thoughts, because he said, "Before you pledge, let's pray."

"Why should I pray?" I thought. "I'm in debt now so deep I'll never get out. Besides, I'll never see a hundred dollars again. Why should I waste my time and God's time?"

I believe everyone in that tent, except me, prayed. I stood erect while all others prayed. I should have had the courtesy, at least, to bow my head during the prayer. But I didn't, and while I stood there, the voice that took my two dollars came to me again. It said, "You! Pledge one hundred dollars."

"Now just a minute! Hold on, fellow! Whoa!" Following that under-breath monologue, I thought, "Why am I getting so excited? He was talking to the fellow behind me, and I caught the voice as it was going by." I turned around, and the young man behind me was having himself a revival. He had both hands in the air and was speaking in tongues.

I thought maybe it was the man in front of me. It wasn't. He also was enjoying an exhilarating time praising the Lord.

I know the Bible says, "My sheep know my voice." But I wasn't taking any chances. God knew He was dealing with a goat, because He put another thought in my mind. "If God spoke to me, He also spoke to Julie, who is only eleven chairs away." I turned my body completely around—I still could not turn my head—and Julie looked up just enough to give me a hundred-dollar smile and nod. That did it. I raised my hand. The evangelist lost me. I never heard a word of his message; not one solitary word.

Guess who came into the tent? The sympathizer! Old Satan with his sly ways came up to me. I didn't know he attended revivals. He stood shoulder to shoulder with me and said, "Isn't it terrible?" I said, "Yes, it is." I started listening to him, and he made sense. He asked me, "Isn't it just awful when you're down and out and have nothing, and God is taking off your very hide?" I agreed.

Satan continued, "You know, you came here tonight to get healed."

"That's right."

"But you didn't get healed. You couldn't even get into the prayer line. Instead, you're out $102. You feel worse. You hurt all over, don't you?" I had to admit I did. We almost had our arms around each other; two buddies. The tempter was tempting.

Suddenly, I recognized this sympathizer for who and what he was; a sneak, a thief, and a liar. I haven't been on speaking terms with him since.

I drove those miles across the desert that night to my home with unbearable pains wracking every part of my body. I had to drive with one arm and hand. I couldn't use the other. I had to stop many times to relax and build up enough strength and courage to go on. It had been over a year since the accident. I staggered into the house about one-thirty in the morning. I had quit for the first time in my life. I never dreamed that I would ever encounter such a time. Why be a quitter? I had never been a quitter. But I knew now I had reached the end of the line.

"Lord, I'm through," I said. "I can't go on. God, where are You? My God, my God, where are You?" God was a million miles away as far as I was concerned. I knew my prayer was not getting through to Him, but I continued pleading.

"My God, I need a touch from You. I need a blessing for my soul. I know I can't reach You. I know it. But God, who shall I call upon to reach You for me?"

God spoke. He said, "Demos Shakarian! He will pray for you."

I didn't know Demos Shakarian. I called the telephone operator and gave the name to her. She had heard of this wonderful Holy Spirit anointed dairy owner and founder of the Full Gospel Business Men's Fellowship International. She put the call through.

When God acts, He always sets the scene first. He had Demos sitting by his telephone when the bell rang. When he answered, I said, "Brother Shakarian, this is Frank Foglio. Sir, I need help."

"How much do you need?"

"Sir, a million dollars wouldn't help me. I need a touch from God. I need a blessing in my soul. I need to feel a blessing from God."

"Hold on, Frank. I'll pray for you."

He prayed the simplest prayer I ever heard. He said, "Oh, God!" As those words were uttered, I felt the doors of heaven open to me. He continued, "Frank is Your son, God. He loves You. God, bless him good. Bless him now from the top of his head to the bottoms of his feet."

The power of God came over me like a mighty tidal wave. It was similar to my experience as a twelve-year-old boy when the power of the Holy Spirit filled me. Blessing came like fine rain. I don't know a thing about the former or the latter rain, or about tomorrow's rain. I only know that I received it all. Wave after wave of fine rain went through my body from the top of my head to the bottoms of my feet. I began speaking in tongues, glorifying the name of the Lord, praising God. The power of God was roaring through my body, and I staggered all over the house praising God.

A Chain of Miracles

A Chain of Miracles

I truly thought I had been healed while the power of the Holy Spirit infilled me. But that old fellow, Satan, the sympathizer who talked to me at the Oral Roberts meeting, put in an appearance. He is always stirring up strife between man and God, using his evil spirit and power wherever he can get a wedge established for a beachhead. He said, "Move your head, Foglio." I couldn't. "Bend over at the waist." It was impossible. "Raise your right arm." Nothing doing.

"Wait a minute," I said. "I'm on speaking terms with God, now." I took advantage of it. "Oh, God, hear me. Listen to me, God. Please hear me out now. Don't ever leave me again."

A broken body is nothing. I'd rather go through life with both legs crippled and one arm missing than to go through life without the blessings of God in my soul. You may never know what it's like to have a deep hunger in your soul that food cannot satisfy. That's what happens when the Lord is not to be found. The blessings you took for granted are not there anymore. It's something you can't imagine. Don't ever leave the Lord. If I am ever able to convince you of anything, let it be this: regardless of your trials and tribulations, don't ever separate yourself from the Lord.

I said, "Lord, if I've got to be crippled the rest of my life, You've got a deal. I'm satisfied. Just keep me anointed. I don't care if I speak in tongues seven days a week. I don't care if I never speak anything. Just stay close to me. I don't mind if I cannot raise my hand to touch You. I only want to feel Your presence and know You are beside me. I can't do without You again. I've arrived. I've come back. I never should have left You. No matter how deep the valley, I want to feel You near."

I had not known what it was to sleep for any length of time for months and months. I took tranquilizers until I reached the point of addiction. I couldn't sleep because each night I would relive the accident. As soon as I fell asleep, I would hear the glass crashing. I'd wake up screaming. But after Demos Shakarian prayed for me, and I received the blessing from the Lord, I slept peacefully each night. I was ready to meet Jesus anytime. It didn't make any particular difference to me when He might call me home, except there remained some unfinished business here upon this earth.

The meat-processing company tottered on the verge of bankruptcy, and we were about to lose our home, our car, everything. Julie got a job to pay the utilities. I decided I had better do something. I could talk, even though my walk was unsteady and sometimes downright clumsy. I suffered periodic dizzy spells which also slowed me considerably. Despite these infirmities, I managed to induce a real-estate broker to sponsor my enrollment in a real-estate school. I graduated and went immediately to my sponsor.

His opening remarks after I walked into his office were, "Son, I hate to discourage you." He hesitated thoughtfully and continued with, "But we're in a real-estate depression. I think you should forget real estate and try something else."

"But you sponsored me."

"I'm sorry I did. No one is selling anything."

I turned to walk out of the office. The Lord spoke to me. "Go on in," he said. I turned back to the man and asked for a chance. Possibly he judged from my appearance I was undergoing a depression of my own.

"Oh, all right," he said. "It's up to you."

The first week I sold a lot for $1500. I almost had a revival in that office. The following week I sold a little house way back in the woods somewhere for $5500.

Things had gotten so bad before I received my first commission check that I had only one suit and that was getting real thin; not in the knees from kneeling in prayer, but above the knees and to the rear. My shoes also were wearing out. One day while walking across the lawn, I felt my feet soaking up water. Both shoes had holes in the soles. I knew what to do, having been raised on a farm. I picked up some good cardboard, took a pair of scissors, cut out two pieces shaped and sized to fit inside my shoes and placed them in there. Those cardboards made the shoes feel real good.

The Lord keeps His eye on the sparrow, and this Italian was the sparrow. God was preparing to do something for me. An architect in New York City, approximately three thousand miles away, had ordered a pair of custom-made shoes, one of the finest brands on the market. He had his feet X-rayed and the shoes were designed to fit perfectly his 10-D size. One day the store called and told him the shoes were ready.

He told his wife the day was so beautiful that he would walk down the Manhattan street to the store, pick up his custom-made shoes and wear them back to the apartment. He arrived at the store, tried on the shoes, and the comfort he experienced delighted him. He started walking home, whistling along the way with happiness. Suddenly something began to happen. The shoes became tight. He loosened the laces. That didn't help. Blisters began to form on his heels and the tops of his big toes. He reached his apartment limping badly and screamed to his wife, "Honey, come quickly. Pull these shoes off my feet. I've blisters on my heels and toes."

"I don't understand," she said. "They were made for your feet. They're expensive. Custom-built."

"Certainly they were made for me. But they don't fit. They hurt me. I don't understand it, either."

"Take them back."

"I will not. I'll never go in that store again."

"But what about the shoes?"

"They're 10-D. They'll fit my brother-in-law, Johnny Sarracino, in Burgettstown, Pennsylvania. I'll send them air-mail, special delivery."

Yes, God had His eye on this Italian sparrow, and He doesn't waste any time when there is a need. When the brother-in-law opened the package, he almost went out of his mind with happiness when he saw those custom-built shoes. They were just his size. He put them on, laced them up and began walking across the living room. They flopped on his feet like oversized bedroom slippers.

He decided the only proper thing to do was mail the shoes to his brother in Fontana, California, who happens to be my brother-in-law. The shoes arrived. My brother-in-law opened the box and almost fainted. He had never seen such beautiful shoes, and they were a gift from his brother. They were just his size—10-D. He slipped his feet into the shoes, laced them up, and started walking around the room. They flopped on his feet as they had with his brother. He went to the shoemaker and bought shoeliner, put it in the shoes, and they flopped worse than before.

God had His eye on the sparrow.

I was sitting in the living room when my brother-in-law arrived. He threw the shoes at me. "You're the only guy I can think of that these shoes might fit," he said, still upset because they didn't fit his feet.

"Put them on," he said. He turned around, and I could see the shoeliner in his pocket. I knew. If the shoes were loose on me, he would sell me the shoeliner.

"New shoes," I exclaimed, looking them over. "And the best brand, too. Praise God! Hallelujah!"

"Try 'em on before you start praising the Lord," he said.

I put them on, and they just snuggled around my feet. I laced them up and walked back and forth.

"How do they feel?"

"Wonderful! Praise God!"

"They don't hurt you? They're not loose? They're not tight?"

"No! Perfect fit."

All I heard as the door slammed was, "I don't understand it." I did. God had His eye on a man with a need, and He supplied that need.

When the commission checks came in for my first real-estate sales, I purchased new shoes and gave the custom-built ones to my pastor. He wore them until he grew tired of them and passed them on to his son who did the same. The last I heard of those shoes, they were in Africa. Some missionary had worn them for a while and passed them on to another missionary. They went traveling all over the world for Jesus.

God knows how to bless you. Sometimes you pray for a million dollars, but God knows you couldn't handle it and would backslide and leave Him forever. God knows how to trust you, too. He knows whether you are tuned in to Him. Thank God, I was back in His fold and really tuned in to His will for me. Every time He spoke, I was ready to move. Ready to act! I was an obedient child.

One afternoon God said to me, "Drive down to the other end of town. There is a big real-estate office there. You go there." I got in my car and drove down there. I was not surprised to see the real-estate office, because God had told me it was there. But He didn't tell me what to do. He probably knew a grown man would not drive there and just sit in his car and look at the building. I didn't.

I walked inside, and way down at the other end of a vast room a man sat at his desk. He had his hat on and was smoking a big black cigar. He looked up, gave me a quick glance, then looked down at the desk, ignoring me completely.

"Lord, are You sure You want me here?" I asked.

Foolish question! Of course He wanted me here, or He would not have sent me. I walked up to the man's desk. "Hi! I'm Frank Foglio."

The only reply was something which sounded like a grunted "Ugmm!" He gave me one of the meanest scowls I ever remember seeing on anyone's face.

"Oh! Oh! Lord!" I said to myself. "You better say something. This guy is going to whip me."

"How's business?" I asked, hoping for an opening wedge to an amiable conversation.

"Rotten! In fact, it's so bad . . . Look at all these listings." He threw a fistful of cards down on his desk. He said, "I can't sell a one, and they're all good ones."

When he slammed down those cards, one listing just floated across the desk and landed in front of me. I picked it up and saw the $95,000 figure. I threw it down, too. "My goodness," I said, "$95,000! Whoever would buy that?"

"Henry Kaiser, and I don't think he could afford it."

God began to work. On the man's desk, underneath the glass, was a little newspaper clipping. It was about two by three and too far away for me to read. The name on that clipping began to rise, and I thought I was getting one of my dizzy spells. I grabbed hold of the corner of the desk. That name rose up so that I was able to read it. Then, the Lord spoke. "He will buy it."

"I've got a buyer! I've got a buyer!" I shouted.

"Where? Where, man? I don't see anyone."

"Right on that paper clipping under the glass on your desk."

We both had to get our noses on the glass to read the name and address, because even though the name had risen up so I could read it, in my excitement I had forgotten it.

"It'll mean a long-distance call," I cautioned.

"Call anywhere if you can sell that property."

I went to the phone, sat down, gave the operator the man's name and address, and she reached him. God always sets the scene when He has us do something. Otherwise, He wouldn't tell us to do it. The man had just arrived from a great revival in New York City. He had walked into the house as the telephone was ringing. He hadn't even set down his suitcase, I learned later.

"Sir! This is Frank Foglio. I have fifty-five acres . . . "

"Just a minute. I know all about that fifty-five acres. While I was in New York City, God spoke to me. He told me to come out there and buy it. So much down." He named the terms. "$95,000. Go ahead. Put it in escrow. I'll send you a check. I'll buy it. You've just sold it."

I put the phone down and still had my hand on the receiver when the realtor, still puffing on the cigar, said, "Huh! Sure cut you off in a hurry, didn't he?"

I turned around in the swivel chair, and I guess I was about as white as his white shirt. I tried to talk, but all that would come out sounded like, "Gong! Gong! Gong!"

"Boy! He certainly scared you!"

I stood up. "Sir! He bought it."

His cigar went "Schruuum!" It flew like a guided missile halfway across the office. "You didn't say a word."

"God sold it."

"He doesn't work here."

"He just got hired."

That big fellow who I thought was so mean got up and put a hand on my shoulder. Big tears rolled down his cheeks. He took my hand and said, "Frank, you don't know what this means to me. I can't make payments on my furniture. I can't make payments on my car. I can't pay my bills at the stores. I'm in bad shape."

"Shake hands with a buddy."

"Would you come to work for me, Frank?"

"Yes, sir. Under one condition. That I may bring my Bible with me to the office and read it here. That I may pray when I feel like praying, and if I feel like saying 'Hallelujah,' I'll say it."

"I'll join you."

We Christians are the biggest cowards in the world. God has said, "Prove Me. Prove Me. And I will pour out a blessing upon you that you cannot contain." And we eke out our pennies. He says, "Give unto Me that which is Mine, and I will give it back to you pressed down and running over."

Read in II Corinthians 9:8 (Amplified Bible): "And God is able to make all grace (every favor and earthly blessing) come to you in abundance, so that you may always and under all circumstances and whatever the need, be self-sufficient—possessing enough to require no aid or support and furnished in abundance for every good work and charitable donation."

Why should we be cowards when, as Christians, we ought to claim the blessings which are rightfully ours through the promise of God? Claim them as children of God.

I went to work for that real-estate broker for whom God sold the fifty-five acres for $95,000. One afternoon, shortly after that sale, he asked me to go down the street and appraise a mansion. I had never appraised anything in my life. I couldn't appraise a doghouse or chicken coop. However, I felt it was God's leading and did not question my ability.

I drove down the other end of town and into a big circular driveway. I took one look at that mansion, and my heart practically jumped up into my throat. But if it was of God's leading, what had I to fear? I got out of the car, walked up to the door, and pressed the buzzer. A tall, dignified lady answered the door.

"Good morning. I'm Frank Foglio. I've come to appraise your house, and I don't know a thing about appraising."

"Wonderful! Come right in."

The Lord had set the scene. She took me through the house and appraised it for me. As I was leaving, she reached down into a large stack of magazines, and from the middle of the stack, she pulled out three, old, stained, and torn magazines and put them in my hand.

"You read these. They'll help you."

Back in my office, I started to dump those magazines into the proper receptacle—the wastebasket. Again the Lord spoke. "Hold on! Read them!" I looked more closely and saw they were copies of Oral Roberts' *Abundant Life.*

There still was something wrong with this Italian Christian. I didn't exactly believe in tithing. I had my Scriptures all mixed-up. I thought I was under the law, "Don't let your left hand know what your right is doing." In that sneaky way, I could escape giving to God without having my conscience bother me. But the Lord still was dealing with me when He said, "Read them!"

I picked up the top magazine and opened it. In big, bold letters across the top of a double spread, it read, "YOU CANNOT OUTGIVE GOD." I put that one aside, picked up the next one, opened it toward the back. Big, bold letters popped out at me: "THESE MEN FROM COAST TO COAST HAVE PROVED THAT YOU CANNOT OUTGIVE GOD." I said, "Humph! They're all on giving." But the magazines weren't three consecutive monthly issues. They were several months apart.

I closed that second magazine and peeled down the cover, looking for the index. I wanted to see if all the articles were on giving. But there was no index. Evidently it had been inadvertently omitted. But there was a story about an alcoholic who had been delivered, saved, and filled with the Holy Spirit. After his deliverance, he borrowed several thousand dollars and gave it to the Lord. Later he became the biggest heavy-machinery equipment operator in the country.

The final magazine I didn't open immediately. I meditated a few minutes. I was certain they couldn't all be on giving. I said, "Please, let this one be just on the Bible?" I should have kept my silence, because right on the cover of that issue was an invitation to the reader: "In this issue, read the first of a series of monthly articles on giving." Inside, another double-page spread proclaiming in big, bold letters, "THESE TEN MEN HAVE PROVED THAT YOU CANNOT OUTGIVE GOD."

I read the names. They were men I knew, men like Demos Shakarian and Henry Krause. I started reading their testimonies, and the power of God came upon me. I put aside the three issues, bowed my head, and started to talk to God.

"God, I believe it. But, God, first I am going to give You ME. I am going to give You ME and all I possess—my family, my home, my car, everything. I am not going to give until it hurts but rather until it helps, because it hurts too quickly."

I was as good as my promise. I did give until it helped—helped others in many ways. One day the certified public accountant who audits my books called me over to the desk he uses when working in my office.

"Mr. Foglio, you've made a mistake."

"What do you mean? I've made a mistake!"

"You've given too much to the Lord."

I said, "I've got news for you, Brother. I haven't given enough, and I'm ashamed I haven't."

The Lord was prospering me financially in the real-estate business, but still I had not been healed physically.

Christ's Healing Power

Christ's Healing Power

Spiritually I was doing exceedingly well, but physically I was on a toboggan slide. The insurance company wanted its doctors to examine me. I suppose they wanted to make certain nothing shady was taking place, no false claims. The doctors gave me a very thorough examination and concluded that my condition was extremely serious. They said I would be a cripple the rest of my life. I felt I should retain an attorney for my dealings with the insurance company. Friends advised me to consult attorney Paul Henry, a born-again Christian.

I walked into his office with my arm still in a sling and wrapped in bandages. "Sir, I need your services," I said when his secretary ushered me into his office. "My name is Frank Foglio."

He stood up, extended a friendly handshake, offered me a chair, and when I was seated, he sat down again.

"I think I have heard of your family," was his opening remark. "Aren't you the people who hold prayer meetings every Monday night?"

"Yes."

"You're one of them, aren't you?"

"Yes, sir."

"You believe in healing, how come your arm is in a sling?" Before I could answer, he shot another question at me. "You speak in tongues, too, don't you?"

"Yes, sir." I came here seeking the services of this attorney, I told myself, and he's putting me through the third degree about my religion.

"Yeah! You're one of them, all right. I want to know one thing. You say you have been in an automobile accident."

"Yes."

"Well, I have to be convinced that you are really still physically handicapped as a result of injuries sustained in that accident."

He took me to his physician, and in the process of the examination, I passed out. Both attorney Henry and his physician were convinced of my serious physical condition. The attorney decided to take my case, and he prepared a medical statement. I had to sign the complaint with my left hand.

The concise report on my condition read: "Right arm severely ripped from socket and placed back under general anesthetic. Doctors had hoped joint would knit, so arm would stay in socket if supported by a sling for a while. Support not enough. Arm repeatedly comes out of socket through recurring dislocations.

"Client also suffered severe brain concussion and effects are with him constantly. Suffered injuries to his spine, making it extremely difficult to get around. Bending over an impossibility. Walks slowly with much pain. Has received finest medical care available."

Attorney Henry, in preparing the statement for the trial, took depositions of the parties involved, obtained the medical and hospital records on me, and read all the doctors' reports concerning my injuries. He talked with my next-door neighbors and the drivers of the cars involved. Soon he had the case prepared to his satisfaction.

A congested court calendar kept the case from coming to trial until a year and a half after attorney Henry filed, and two and one-half years after the accident. Two weeks before the trial, the attorney had me examined by the surgeons who had attended me at the time of the accident. He said he wanted a current examination, that the doctors might testify in court concerning permanent disabilities. Injuries normally will heal sufficiently so that after two and one-half years, conclusive evidence is present as to whether injuries will be permanent.

I began to stumble and fall, due to the effects of the injuries, as I walked out of the examining room and into the entrance to the doctors' offices. I suffered headaches and dizzy spells constantly, and a dizzy spell was coming on as I walked down the corridor. The attorney took hold of me on one side and the nurse on the other. They helped me into a chair, and the nurse brought some smelling salts to revive me. I'm certain I passed out, because when I came to, the nurse was waving the smelling salts under my nose.

Julie and I went over to attorney Henry's home the night before the trial was to begin. We were on a first-name basis now. Paul Henry's brother and several others were there, and they decided to have prayer.

"God is alive, and God is still on the business end of meeting human needs on the level of our needs," Paul explained. "Frank needs healing, and I need wisdom and strength as far as this law business is concerned. I know that it is 'not by might, nor by power, but by my Spirit, saith the Lord.' We might paraphrase that and say, 'not by wits, nor by psychiatry, but by my Spirit, saith the Lord.'"

We prayed, putting all things in the hands of the Lord, including the judge, jury, witnesses, doctors—everyone who had any connection with the case. While we were praying, I started talking personally to the Lord. I told the Lord, "Oh, God, if You will heal me, I'll testify for You. I'll testify that You healed me." God didn't see fit to answer my prayer. When I finished praying, it took me about three minutes to get up from kneeling, because of my spinal condition.

The trial got under way Tuesday, September 4, 1957. After the jury was selected, Paul began calling witnesses. He called a police officer who testified concerning physical elements pertaining to the scene—tire skid marks, damaged parts of the vehicles, where the occupants were found in relation to the vehicles, and other pertinent information.

Paul put on witnesses, one after another. My next-door neighbor testified that he had been my neighbor for five years; that prior to the accident I had been very healthy, strong and robust, but for the past two and one-half years, ever since the accident, I had been substantially a cripple. He testified that he had not seen me use any garden tools or pick up or play with my children in two and one-half years. He added that the most work he had seen me do, since the accident, was to hold a garden hose.

The doctor testified that my right arm had been ripped out of the socket, and I had suffered a number of recurring dislocations during the two and one-half years following the accident. He said surgery might alter the condition. He described the operation as requiring approximately a nine-inch incision, laying all the flesh back, and stapling a hinge onto the upper end of the arm bone and to the shoulder bone.

The hinge would keep the bone from coming out of the socket. Then they would lay back the flesh, sew it up, and after an extensive series of physical-therapy treatments, I would regain use of the arm to a limited degree. However, there would be approximately 25 percent limitation of movement in that arm and shoulder, and that would be permanent disability.

As far as the brain concussion was concerned and the after-effects, nothing could be done. It was permanent, and I would have to live with it.

The injury to my spine was beyond medical help. Possibly in the future, if it grew progressively worse, which the doctor estimated would happen, fusion of the joints involved might be necessary.

One of the insurance company's doctors who examined me remained in the courtroom during each session, ready to testify, but his company evidently did not desire his testimony to be heard. God moved in many ways, and on the third day the insurance company offered a settlement, and Paul advised me to accept it.

"Thank God," I said, "the case is over. And thank You, Lord, for a substantial financial blessing." Paul joined me in a prayer of thanksgiving in an anteroom of the courtroom.

I have given the medical explanation of my physical condition in such detail so that there will be no conjectures on the seriousness of my physical disabilities. Even though I had been working in real estate, I was not in good condition physically, and there was little possibility of my improving, except through divine intervention.

Julie and I were so happy over the results of the case that we decided to have a spaghetti dinner in our home and invited many of our friends. I called Demos Shakarian.

"Hello, Brother Demos," I said. "This is Frank Foglio in Fontana."

"Brother Frank, how are you? God bless you."

"Praise the Lord. Demos, my wife and I are inviting some friends to our home September 17 for a spaghetti dinner. We would like to have you join us."

"May I bring Tommy Hicks and Brother Roll and . . . "

"Yes, Demos. Bring your friends." When you invite Demos to an affair, you better be prepared to ask half of Los Angeles, because he usually is accompanied by a host of friends. I had invited my Baptist attorney Paul Henry and his family. Years before, Paul had received the baptism as a young boy, but had "cooled off." Recently, he had been going to the Full Gospel Business Men's Fellowship breakfasts and other meetings, and this association had led him back into a deeper spiritual life. There were several others at the dinner that night, including my mother.

After dinner, we adjourned to the living room, where the conversation drifted around to the big crusade in progress at that time in South America. No one had mentioned healing. Suddenly Paul Henry became spiritually enthusiastic with the idea that I would be healed that evening. He told me about it later.

"Frank," he said, "I was sitting there in your living room, among all those men who really knew God, men who had been in constant contact with God. I felt as though I was sitting among Peter, James, Paul, and John. I received the impression that these men knew God, and they had power from God."

Paul was not a man to sit on ideas. He acted. He jumped to his feet, looked over at me, and said, "Frank, these men could pray for you, and God would heal you." He grabbed a chair and sat it down in the middle of the living room.

"Sit in this chair," he said. "It's an electric chair, full of spiritual electricity."

I sat down. The men gathered around me and began to pray. They laid hands on me, and as they prayed, I began to weep. I had quit praying for a healing long ago, resigning myself to being a cripple the rest of my life.

Suddenly I heard the same voice that said, "Don't do it!" when I was going to take my son with me to San Bernardino. The same voice that said, "You! Give two!" and "You! Pledge one hundred dollars." Now, it was saying to me, "Be still and know that I am God." Then a second time, "Be still and know that I am God."

Seconds later I jumped to my feet, completely delivered by the power of God. I heard every vertebra snapping into place. I felt the pressure released from my brain. I felt my arm pulled back into the socket. I had been set free by the power of the Holy Spirit, liberated by the power of God. All my infirmities were gone.

"I'm healed! I'm healed!" I shouted.

There always are some doubting Thomases among us, and thank God for them, because often they confirm what God has done for us.

Paul Henry asked, "Are you really healed?" Can you imagine that? He was the one who so enthusiastically suggested the prayer for healing.

"I'm healed, Paul. I know it. God has healed me."

"Well! We'll find out." He came over to me and gouged me with his fist in the shoulder where the injury had been.

"See! I'm healed!"

That wasn't enough for Paul. He hit me on the arm that had been slipping out of the socket. He hit it hard, and I said, "I'm healed!"

He asked me if I could touch the floor. I stooped down, bending at the waist, and touched the floor. "Can you raise your arms above your head?" I pushed them upward as far as I could reach. That was it. I had passed the test. Everyone knew I had been healed.

The power of God came upon every individual in that room. Paul began speaking in tongues. Mamma was glorifying God in a beautiful language. Others spoke in tongues. Many languages were represented. We glorified and exalted our Lord, our mighty Deliverer and Liberator, for He had honored our household. He delivered me and set me free at seven o'clock on the evening of September 17, 1957. Ever since that moment, I have not had any recurrence or reminder of pain of any kind connected with the injuries suffered in that automobile accident. I was thoroughly healed physically. But God was not finished with His miracles and with me.

Giving Until It Helps

Giving Until It Helps

I was in Tulsa, Oklahoma, shortly after my healing, attending a Full Gospel Business Men's Fellowship convention. Velmer Gardner was making one of his excellent pleas just before the offering. God uses that man in a mighty way for the work of the Lord. It was as if God had suddenly spoken to him in the midst of his plea, because he stopped talking for a full minute and then said, "There is someone here who is going to give $2,000."

I thought, "That's great. He must have someone in mind." I was certain it couldn't be Frank Foglio, because I had only a few dollars in my pocket and a credit card.

"Let's pray," Velmer Gardner said.

Sure! Let's pray! I can do that. But I didn't. I just sat there, exactly as I did at the Oral Roberts meeting in Bakersfield. Nice way for this Italian to act just after a miraculous healing. While sitting there, not even exercising my prerogative to pray, the Lord spoke to me. He always seemed to be speaking to me regarding financial matters. He said, "You are going to pledge $2,000."

"Wait a minute, Lord. I don't even have two *hundred* dollars."

"You pledge $2,000."

"Lord, you have the wrong man. All these millionaires here—surely one of them will cough up. You watch. You'll get it."

I waited about five minutes, and nothing happened. No one pledged that $2,000. Then Velmer Gardner said, "That man has not pledged it, and God is speaking to his heart now."

Make no mistake about it. God had His finger pointing at me, and I knew it. I pledged and went $2,000 in debt. Shortly afterward, they took a special offering for some special need. Many pledged $600. I figured I was exempt this time around. I already had pledged $2,000 I did not have. But I was wrong again. The Lord spoke. "You pledge $600." That's $2,600 in debt. I came to be blessed. The Lord hadn't blessed me enough with my family and my healing. No! I wanted the heavens to open wide with showers of blessings poured down upon me. Then Gardner put the icing on the cake.

"You pray that within a year the Lord will give it back. If He doesn't, you talk to me."

A year went by and we still had not paid our pledge of $2,600. I said to Julie, "We'd better go pay it." We went out and borrowed on our furniture and paid those pledges. It was pretty rough.

One afternoon shortly afterward, I took the family for a little drive. We were passing a piece of property that I had driven by repeatedly for years. It was some kind of an estate. I couldn't read the owner's name or telephone number on the "for sale" sign hanging on the gate at the entrance to the estate grounds. Probably the illegibility of the printing on the sign was God's way of keeping the property from selling, because as I drove by, the Lord spoke to me. He said, "Buy that property." I slammed on the brakes and almost threw my son and daughter into the front seat with Julie and me. I told Marilyn to get out of the car and write down the name and telephone number on the sign. She did.

"What are you going to do?" Julie asked.

"I'm going to buy it."

"But you only have $75 in the bank."

"Fine! I'm going to buy that estate."

The next day I called the man and explained I wanted to

buy the property. I made a $25 deposit, opened the escrow, and sold the escrow for a $7,000 profit, and I was on my way. God blessed and blessed and blessed. The $2,600 I had pledged and borrowed from the bank to make good my pledge returned me $7,000 on that one transaction. Oh, what God can do if we will only give Him the opportunity. But we eke it out and complain.

"Well, Lord, I gave You $100 last month and You didn't give me a thing."

Go to your doctor and have a physical. You'll probably learn there is nothing wrong with you. Hasn't the Lord given you something? Perfect health? Aren't three meals a day anything? It doesn't bother you after those three full meals to sleep at night. Isn't it worth $100 a month to get a full night's sleep each night of the year? I would say it's worth $1,000. Your nerves are like steel. Your legs are strong. Your eyes are good. And the Lord hasn't given you anything in return for the $100 a month you give Him?

I learned the hard way. You don't have to give until it hurts. You give until it helps, and many times that greatly exceeds tithing. The 10 percent you give in tithing is what the Lord demands. You are not giving to the Lord until you exceed that 10 percent of your income, and the 10 percent comes off the top, not after expenses are deducted. How many friends have you dined with who today tip the waitresses or waiters 15 or 20 percent of the tab because of the present spiraling inflation? What about the Lord? Aren't the costs of doing His work affected by the same inflationary measures? And yet, how many today still are holding to that old 10 percent when it comes to giving to the Lord?

Don't be afraid to step out. Don't think small. Think big and act big. Turn everything over to God. He tells you to ask largely. Ask largely! Not, this, "Oh, Lord, if only I could pay my bills."

Ask big. "Lord, bless me. Cause me to prosper not only spiritually and physically, but financially and materially. Not for me, but for Your glory. All I have is Yours, including my family and me." After you have asked, praise the Lord. Thank Him with praises of thanksgiving for blessing you, not only for blessings of increase but also for adversities. Thank and praise Him for all things.

Don't call the Lord your partner. That's one mistake I made. He's not my partner, He's my boss. I had been going under the assumption for years that He was my partner; in other words, I was telling the world that Jesus is responsible for everything I do, even my mistakes. We all make mistakes. We promise things we know we will be unable to fulfill. If Jesus is your partner, He is responsible for 50 percent of everything that happens to you. You are dragging Him down to your level by claiming Him as your partner. Make Him your boss. Nothing will go wrong when He is running the show.

We try to do God's job. We try to do the impossible instead of committing it to God. What do you have in your hand? Commit that meager bit to God as my mother did with less than a quarter of a pound of spaghetti. She committed it to God, and He blessed it to the extent that it fed eighteen hungry people, and there was enough left over to feed twelve Foglios the next day. Praise God! That's committing and believing. What do you have in your hand? We sit and shake, cry and beg, pleading like unsaved individuals when all we have to do is take what we have and commit it to God. Get down on your knees and commit it to Him. Then stand back. Take your hands off it and let God.

It's time we lock ourselves in our bedrooms or in our offices, alone, and sit down and talk to God. If I came into your office or home, would you start screaming at me like an auctioneer? I wouldn't understand you, and I would become justifiably disgusted. How do you think God feels? He'd like to have a talk with you sometime. Just sit there and say, "Oh, God, You know my heart. You know my life, and my problems. God, unless You help me, I'm helpless. God, I can't think anymore. I can't do anything, and I have no finances. God, I'm tired, and I can't go on. Everything is going wrong. I love You, God. Everything I have is Yours, God. I'll serve You. I won't let You down again. God, bless me! Prosper my soul. You said that You wish above all things that we should prosper and be in health as our souls prosper."

One time in my office I was talking to God in that manner. Suddenly I felt His presence. I felt Him standing by my right elbow, and I was scared to look. I closed my eyes. He spoke to me and told me what to do, and in a matter of minutes all my problems were solved.

God doesn't want any of us to fail. We are failing because we ask amiss. He said, ask largely. Do it and see what God can do. Challenge Him. He will protect and watch over you. He said, "It shall not come nigh to thy dwelling." But you are struggling, trying to do it alone, and you are failing. You want to pay your bills. You want to be current in your financial affairs. You want to protect your credit. You want to keep going. You want to give to God. Yet the devil is constantly wedging in, continually tearing at your foundation. Recognize who he is. Turn him over to God. Plead the Blood on him. "You devil, you, I come against you, not in my name but in the name of Jesus Christ. Lord, kick him around. Lord, You handle him." Then watch yourself go.

The more He blesses you, the more will your faith grow in God. The more He prospers you, the more you will be infilled with the Holy Spirit. The more He gives you, you give back to Him. He will send it back to you in ever-growing amounts, pressed down and running over, as the Bible says. It becomes a never-ending cycle. Just dare to believe God. Dare to witness for Him. He will deliver beyond your wildest dreams.

I almost missed my plane one evening witnessing on the telephone to a businessman who had been prosperous, but at the time I was talking with him he was as broke as anyone could be. I gave it to him straight, telling it like it is. No coddling and speeches of sympathy. Instead, I laid it on the line.

"I can't give," he said.

"Oh, yes you can. Listen to me. I'm going to dictate a letter, and you write it down." I still have a copy of that letter, which reads:

"God, I hereby do pledge to You in the name of Jesus $5,000. I will give it to You and more. You are my supplier. You are my source of supply. You will meet my needs. Sincerely, John Smith."

After I finished dictating the letter, a real revival started on the other end of that line. The businessman began speaking in tongues. I guess he was running all around his living room, because I couldn't reach him for a while. Finally he returned to the telephone and said, "I am going to airmail, special delivery, this letter to you." I received the letter and placed it where I can refer to it periodically. I am already enjoying the pleasure of seeing this man blessed out of his debt-ridden life.

Things began to happen to me in a tremendous way after I trusted God and promised Him my whole life. I told God that I had an appointment to take an elderly man out to lunch. We can't ignore older people. They want company. They like to talk to people. They are human.

The elderly gentleman was wealthy. But I told the Lord I was not taking him out because of his money. No! I loved the man. We went to lunch, and he picked up the tab. After lunch he wanted to visit, hungrily desiring companionship. He also enjoyed riding, so we rode on one of the freeways in his chauffeur-driven limousine. Discreetly, I had steered the conversation to a discussion of man's soul, and how he needed to accept Jesus Christ as his Savior, when like a bolt out of the blue, my friend said, "Brother Foglio, I don't know why I am telling you this, but I have thirty-one acres of land in Los Angeles. It's ten minutes from City Hall. I'm old, and it's going to còst me a quarter of a million dollars in estate taxes to die. I want to move that property. Too much land and too many taxes."

Thirty-one acres of land within ten minutes of City Hall! Glory be to God! Hallelujah! I wanted to stand up in the back seat of that limousine, raise my hands heavenward, and shout praises to the Lord. I knew I had a buyer. No problem moving that property. The Lord had told me who to call the moment my friend said he wanted to move the property. I called the man as soon as I arrived at my office. I had sold him quite a bit of real estate, and he trusted me. When I told him about the thirty-one acres in Los Angeles, he said, "I'll take it." He didn't bother to look at the property; instead, he came to my office and looked at the location of the land on a map of the Los Angeles area.

"What do you think of it?"

"Wonderful! Just wonderful!"

I could hardly contain my ecstasy. Not because it meant a big commission for me; far beyond the realization of any material gains, it meant a sizable contribution for the work of the Lord.

We've been too stingy with God. We're in the shape we are in not because of God but because of ourselves. The Bible tells us, "He maketh a way where there seemeth no way." How many times have we been there? The devil wants us to quit. He tried to persuade me to quit when I returned from the Oral Roberts crusade in Bakersfield. He sneaks up on us at the opportune moment, when we think all is lost. There is no such thing as quitting; no such thing as giving up and lying back and dying. Absolutely not!

The devil wants to whisper to you and say, "Look! He said He would bless and prosper you. But look at what you have. You are not getting anything back. Look at what you gave in tithing last year. What did you receive in return? False promises."

My God shall supply "all your need according to his riches in glory by Christ Jesus" (Phil. 4:19). He will not fail. He said, "I never shall forsake nor leave thee." Then who is leaving whom? The devil watches us. He knows when to hit. It's usually when we are feeling high and happy and everything is going fine. Our bars are down. Prosperity has caused us to backslide a little, which allows the devil to slip in his wedges; therefore, when we are at our best and God is supplying every need, that is the time to shout and praise and glorify God, and get deep in the Spirit. Thank Him for everything. Don't relax for a single moment.

Pray in English. Pray in Yugoslav. Pray in Italian. God has warned us that Satan is not stupid. He knows every language of the universe. He knows every dialect. There is not a language he cannot speak and interpret. We had better become educated in the Holy Spirit and speak in the Spirit. When we do that, we confuse old split-hoof.

Instead of saying, "God, I'm in trouble. I'm in a hole, $22,000 in a hole," pray, "Oh, sahra, karenda kio mio," which means, "Lord, I'm 22,000 in the red." The devil doesn't even know what you have said. It upsets him so that he goes back into his pit and hides in a corner.

Pray in the Spirit while driving down the road or through city traffic. In your heart, pray in the Spirit. In your office, talking to a businessman, talk to Him in your heart and pray in the Spirit. You will win many points. The Lord will bless you. Never make any move, whether you are a businessman or a salaried employee—or whatever your station in life—without first having a good prayerful session with the Lord. It will pay dividends.

The Lord not only prospers us spiritually, but also physically, mentally, materially, and financially. Sometimes His blessings appear to us to be adversities. Actually, He is blessing us in a way that at the time we do not understand.

A few years after my healing, I met a Christian man whose resigned impoverishment so annoyed me that I decided to show him how, through God's blessings, he could overcome his poverty. We were riding from Fontana to Los Angeles in this gentleman's car, a truly old model. He lived in a little old shack of a house with his wife and five children. He called himself a businessman, but even such a distinction for him was dubious. On the ride to Los Angeles, that old car spit and sputtered and so much smoke came up through the floorboards that I rode with my head out the window to escape asphyxiation. Motoring to Los Angeles and back to Fontana, we blew out three tires. I became furious.

"Brother," I said, "you have no business living like a defeated poor man. You're saved and filled with the Holy Spirit. Go out and borrow $10,000 and bring it to me at my office."

I guess the Lord must have been using some pretty strong language through me. We took our motor trip on Saturday and the following Monday he called me. He was scared. He said he hadn't slept for two nights.

"I have the $10,000," he announced. "You come and get it." His voice actually quivered. He must have mortgaged everything he had. But he was cautious, as I soon learned. When I arrived at his house, he had two promissory notes made out. He said, "Brother Foglio, I feel I shouldn't take a chance for the whole amount. You sign this note." He handed me one of the two notes and said, "You take responsibility for five, and I will accept responsibility for five."

I took the $10,000 check and returned to my office. A few days later I saw a piece of ground, and the Lord told me to buy it for my friend and myself. I bought it and short-termed it out. The transaction returned an $8,000 profit, four of which I sent to my friend. A short time later, I picked up another piece of property and made $15,000. On and on the buying and selling went. Odd as it may seem with these turnovers, I had to battle this man every inch of the way. I had to drag him by the heels that he might be blessed by the Lord.

I bought a parcel of land with a down payment of twenty-five hundred dollars. The parcel consisted of 4½ acres for

$27,250, and I told my friend to hold it until I said to sell. Every time we wanted to sell, the Lord checked me, even when my friend had an offer of $35,000 for it. He really wanted to unload and take his profit. But he waited.

Then one day, while I was on my knees in prayer, the Lord told me a buyer would make a bid for my friend's parcel and he should sell. I called him and gave the go-ahead to sell. A few days later he called, so filled with excitement he could hardly talk. "Guess what?" he shouted.

"You've sold!"

"Yep! I'm in escrow at 75,000 cash!"

God has blessed that man tremendously. Had you known him before these transactions with me and met him today you would not know he was the same man. He has tremendous faith and is a great soul-winner. He proved God. He dared to step out. Ask largely and believe, and you will receive.

The Bible says in III John 2: "I wish above all things that thou mayest prosper and be in health, even as thy soul prospereth." Believe. It's not a sin to make a dollar. Make it, but use it for God. You can't out-give God. Try it.

While God's blessings were falling upon me like spring showers, some clouds began appearing on the horizon. The years since my healing had seen me prosper, but there were spiritual vacuums about me which needed filling.

Home To Glory

Home to Glory

God had been tremendous in the lives of the members of our family, led by a little mother who dared to believe, who dared to serve God fearlessly against all opposition, like a commander in chief leading her little pack as she did back in those early days when she went from door to door witnessing in a number of towns. It was Mamma who kept us together through the years, and she never missed having a weekly prayer meeting in our home since that first one in the farmhouse in Raccoon, Pennsylvania, in 1926. But her life had its mountain peaks of joy and valleys of despair despite her complete dedication to her Lord.

One of her griefs centered on my brothers Joe, Fred, and Carmen and my brother-in-law, Jimmy Sarracino. They had not received the baptism in the Holy Spirit, although each had received Jesus Christ into his heart.

My oldest brother, Joe, was lukewarm toward Christianity and more interested in making money than getting the baptism in the Holy Spirit. A successful businessman in Weirton, West Virginia, Joe visited us in Fontana as often as freedom from business pressures permitted. Mamma would tell him very sweetly, "Joe, you better get filled with the Holy Spirit. You better change your ways." Joe always gave the same answer. He would reach into his pocket, take out his wallet, pat it affectionately and say, "Mamma, this is my God."

Mamma patted him on the face but never uttered a word of criticism. She tried to talk to Carmen, who was bitter over Tony being captured and killed by the enemy in World War

II. Like Fred, he would not listen to Mamma. Jim Sarracino expressed satisfaction with merely being saved. But Mamma wasn't satisfied. She zeroed in on Joe, Carmen, and Jim, setting her alarm clock for three each morning and getting out of bed to pray for the three boys. I can remember hearing her talk with God.

"Hey God! You fill Joe with the Holy Spirit. You fill Carmen with the Holy Spirit. You fill Jim with the Holy Spirit. Thank You, God." She made simple but powerful prayers.

One year, Joe visited us during a revival in Ontario, California. Mamma wanted him to go to the revival with her. She asked Carmen and Jim, also, to come along. Joe agreed to go, but made it plain he was going only to please Mamma. We went to the revival and heard Bernie Davis, a powerful man in the Lord. Frankly, I was scared. I thought, "Oh, God, I hope nothing happens to upset Joe." You know how we are sometimes, trying to tell God how to run our lives or a church service, filled with fear, running ahead of God. I said, "God, I hope some little old lady doesn't burst forth in tongues or scream and squall. It surely will drive Joe away."

We sat there listening to Bernie Davis, and I was tense. Joe was sitting beside me, dignified and well-dressed, the epitome of an affluent businessman, self-satisfied and smug. The service moved along, and I grew more apprehensive. We invite trouble when we began fearing it will strike us. Like a magnet, we draw to us that which we fear. I should have heeded the advice in II Tim. 1:7, "For God hath not given us the spirit of fear; but of power, and of love, and of a sound mind."

The evangelist was nearing the end of his sermon when the power of God hit a little, sixteen-year-old girl. She leaped to her feet, began speaking in tongues, and fell in the aisle. That upset Joe. I grabbed him by the arm to keep him from leaving. He even cursed, and I thought of Eph. 4:30, "Grieve not the holy Spirit."

"You people are insane. You're out of your minds," Joe intoned in my ear. "I don't believe any of this. It's all psychosomatic reaction." I managed to calm him down. After the service, Bernie Davis showed Joe so much love and spoke with such enthusiasm about Mamma and what a faithful servant she was to the Lord that Joe was deeply impressed. Bernie said he was moving to Chino for a revival meeting there. He invited Joe to come over and bring the family.

"Yeah! I'll be there," Joe answered.

His word was his bond. When he made a promise, he kept it. I knew this about Joe, but it did surprise me the following night when he mentioned the meeting. "All right," he said. "Let's all get in my car and drive over to Chino to hear Bernie Davis."

Again I prayed, "Oh, God, let everything go well." I didn't know, but I might have suspected that in the background Mamma was talking to God in her own conversational manner. "Hey God! You fill my boys with the Holy Spirit. Thank You, God."

We drove up in Joe's big car at the address of the church and what I saw shook me. We were in front of an old store building that looked as though it should have been condemned by building inspectors years ago. We walked inside and were confronted with plain, old wooden benches put together with one-by-twelve planks. The benches and floor were dusty. We sat down, Joe in his dapper gray suit looking as much out of place as a king in a fisherman's shanty or a pauper in a palace.

"My God! My God!" I agonized. "Why did You let us come here?"

God sets the scene. We worry and fret because we are of the flesh. "For they that are after the flesh do mind the things of the flesh; but they that are after the Spirit the things of the Spirit" (Rom. 8:5).

The Holy Spirit energized the singing. I could feel the

service moved along smoothly with Bernie preaching a dynamic sermon on the baptism in the Holy Spirit. When he had finished, Bernie asked that every head be bowed, and then he gave the altar call. I kept my head bowed for a few minutes, and then I looked up. Joe was gone! I knew what had happened. He had slipped out for a smoke and probably would be sitting in the car, waiting for us when we came out. Poor Joe!

I turned my attention to a group of men standing in a circle at the front of the church. One of the men turned and motioned to me to join the group. I went forward and found Joe flat on his back on the floor and covered with dust from the top of his head to the bottoms of his feet, his beautiful gray suit hopelessly wrinkled and dirty where he had rolled around on the floor. He had kicked one shoe off and was trying to get to his feet. He would brace his hands on the floor and raise himself slightly, then drop back again, hitting the floor with a solid blow. He repeated his efforts several times, but each ended in failure. No one touched him. Finally, he quit the struggle, lay flat on his back and relaxed. The power of God came upon him and he was saved and baptized in the Holy Spirit.

When will we learn that " . . . man looketh on the outward appearance, but the Lord looketh on the heart" (I Sam. 16:7)?

Joe finally got to his feet, reached into his pocket, pulled out a package of cigarettes and stomped the package to pieces with his stockinged foot. During Joe's infilling with the Holy Spirit, my brother Carmen was saved and also filled with the Spirit.

Joe and Carmen spoke in tongues and praised the Lord during the drive home and all that night. Jim became excited and jealous because he didn't receive the baptism, but the next night, at Mamma's prayer meeting, he, too, came under the power and was filled with the Holy Spirit. Mamma was in her glory. She continually walked about the house with a grin from ear to ear saying, "Hey, God. You fill my boys with the Holy Spirit. Thank You, God."

The transformation which occurred in Joe's life astounded everyone who knew him. He returned to Weirton and became a powerhouse for God. Every night after he left his office, he got into his light air coupe and flew to such cities as Pittsburgh, Steubenville, Cleveland, Columbus, and other areas in West Virginia, Ohio, and Pennsylvania to witness for Jesus Christ and relate the story of his salvation. His work for the Lord continued for three years, never missing a day of testifying somewhere for his Lord and Savior. His tremendous enthusiasm and energy reminded me of Mamma, and how, after being saved and filled with the Holy Spirit, she traveled from one town to another, knocking on doors and explaining, "I want to tell you about Jesus."

Joe's testimony brought hundreds of souls to the Lord. He labored in the Lord's vineyard day and night, never tiring, always hurrying—hurrying as though there was too little time left for him to tell others about Jesus. It may have been a premonition which drove him.

One day, three years after his baptism in the Holy Spirit, he took off from the Weirton airport with a Roman Catholic priest for a short flight to Sewickley, Pennsylvania. During the flight, the plane engine began to heat up. He landed at Aliquippa and remained there until the engine cooled, and took off again. The plane began losing altitude shortly after the takeoff and before long, it crashed. The priest, who had grown fond of Joe and was responding to his testimony, escaped with a few minor scratches and bruises. Joe suffered fractures of both jaws and arms, mangled legs, and ten broken ribs, one penetrating a lung.

I received a telephone call in Fontana from Joe's wife. She said I had better hurry. Joe had been calling for me and was in bad shape. My brother Fred and I flew to Aliquippa, where we remained at Joe's bedside for five days. Joe was conscious when we arrived, but soon thereafter lapsed into a coma.

Instead of screaming in pain and agony, he continually repeated, "Glory to God! Glory to God!" We tried to talk to him, but he did not hear us or, at least, he didn't seem to comprehend what we were saying, except when I talked about Jesus or said, "Praise the Lord." Then he would smile, his face radiating joy.

The fifth day after the accident, Joe went home to the Lord. He went out of this world glorifying his Savior and leaving behind a great harvest of saved souls. Thank God, for "By their fruits ye shall know them" (Matt. 7:20).

I called Mamma, and all I could say was, "Mom! Mom! Mom!" I couldn't tell her that Joe had gone to be with Jesus. But she knew.

"Son, it's not good. Is it?"

"No, Mamma."

"Bring him home."

We took the body back to Fontana. Mamma, weeping and sobbing, walked by the casket. She didn't become angry with God for taking her son to be with Him. She knew this was God's will, and she thanked God that Joe had done so well for his Lord.

"I see you some day soon," she told Joe as the casket was lowered in the grave.

Mamma was growing old and tired. I could observe the telltales, but I didn't want to believe them. This year, 1965, had been especially burdensome to her, with Joe's accident and death draining much of her strength. But this year also marked the thirty-ninth anniversary of a continuous weekly prayer meeting each Monday night in our home, starting in the farmhouse in Raccoon, Pennsylvania. We went forward with plans for the observance. Mamma invited all the saints of God from the Fontana area and all the members of our family. She made a special plea to my brother Fred, who was born in the farmhouse the year the prayer meetings were started by Mamma.

Fred is around five-feet-seven, and his hair is totally white.

He served as a deputy in the sheriff's department. Fred is a very brave individual, a person who lives strictly according to his own whims. He didn't care too much about getting totally involved with God once he had grown to manhood, but he was quite different in his younger days.

Fred was saved, filled with the Holy Spirit, and spoke in tongues when he was only seven years old. He became one of the greatest miracles of salvation I ever saw in a child. Then he joined the Navy when he was eighteen years old, and the picture changed. He began to drink and smoke heavily and developed a serious case of ulcers. Surgeons removed 60 percent of his stomach. He asked us to come to the hospital and have prayer with him. God graciously brought him through the operation and returned him to normal health, but the blessings failed to touch him. He continued his own pattern of living.

He did come to our home the night Mamma celebrated the thirty-ninth anniversary of our prayer meetings. He walked into the house with a big cigar in his mouth and greeted Mamma with a "Hi, Mamma!" and blew smoke in her face. Mamma never said a word, just kept that twinkle in her eyes. She never hit or whipped any of her children. Her hands were soft as velvet and, instead of hitting any of us, she would take one of her little hands and pat us on the cheek and smile. There were times when she did that to me, and I wished she had hit me with a club, because that little pat on the face brought terrible conviction on me as it did with my brothers and sisters. She seemed to know exactly how we were living without being told.

The anniversary prayer meeting was attended by about seventy-five people. I had been in charge of prayer meetings periodically since I was twelve years old. I took charge of this service and led the singing. Fred outsang everyone, shouting at the top of his lungs. Mamma sat in her little corner, as usual in later years, quietly praising the Lord in the Spirit. We knelt down at prayer time, and the presence of the Lord filled the room with everyone praising the Lord and speaking in tongues—just a sincere, Spirit-filled Pentecostal meeting.

Out of the corner where Mamma sat, suddenly came the familiar voice and phrase, "Hey God!" The prayer meeting came to a complete stop, not a whisper. The "Hey God!" shut off all the shouting, silenced every voice.

Mamma took charge. She said, "Hey God! My boy Fred. He's here tonight. You know, God, when he was seven years old he was saved and filled with the Holy Spirit. But God, now he's backslid. You know, God. He's here. He's right over there."

Fred began to shake so badly that the chair he sat in started to rattle, sounding like a .30-caliber machine gun, there was such conviction in his bones. He didn't know whether to stay or run out the door. I think, if it hadn't been for the embarrassment, he would have run all the way home.

Mamma continued to pray. "Lord, You know. You gotta bring him back. Yes, God. You bring him back. I thank You. Amen."

Fred went up to Mamma after the prayer meeting. He was so mad and so confused he could hardly talk. He sputtered over a few words and then said, "Mamma, don't you ever talk to God like that again. I'll never come back here."

Mamma smiled, patted him on the cheek and said, "You nice boy."

Fred became so confused he didn't know what to say or do. His perplexity did not surprise Mamma, who knew that someday her prayers would be answered, no matter how long it would take.

One day not many weeks later, Mamma called my sister Jessie on the telephone. "I want you to listen to me. You write down everything I tell you."

She told Jessie all the things she wanted done and exactly how. She explained the type of casket she wanted to be buried in, the type of dress she wanted to wear, and who was to be at the funeral service as far as preachers were concerned. She named the songs to be sung.

"There is to be no crying, because you know where Mamma has gone." She added, "I'm to go home pretty soon. Going to see Costy, Tony, Joe, and Dad. I'm going to be leaving."

Little did we realize Mamma was tired, worn out, and very shortly would be with our brothers and dad. The doctors had told us that all she needed was a rest, a little building up. But I could tell Mamma was longing for heaven. She was tired. She had fought a good fight. She wanted to see Jesus and her loved ones who had gone on before her.

Jessie wrote down everything Mamma told her. She was a sweet little woman and didn't question Mamma. Mamma didn't call me to come and listen to what she had to say, because even if I believed it, she knew I would laugh and try to turn it lightly aside. That was my way. But Mamma knew. She had set her house in order, made her will, and made it so foolproof—guided by the Holy Spirit—that no member of the family had any comments to make.

Mamma went outside the house after she finished talking with Jessie. She noticed a man walking up the street, and the Lord told Mamma to witness to him. She never failed to give her testimony when the opportunity presented itself, and if an opportunity did not arise, she would make one. She stumbled alongside the house, pressed against it for support, and managed to get to the gate as the stranger approached.

"Sir!" She hailed him. "You better accept Christ and accept Him quickly. You haven't got long."

"I won't hear it," the man replied.

"I want to tell you about Jesus."

"I don't want to hear it."

Four days later, I went to that man's funeral. He had his chance.

My sister Dolly visited Mamma the day after she tried to witness to the stranger. She told Dolly about the experience. Mamma was lying on her bed, and when she finished with her story she said, "I'm a little tired. You go away a little bit and let me rest."

Dolly hesitated. "You don't look too well," she told Dolly. "You go home. Come back. See me later."

Dolly stepped out of the room, and Mamma just stole away to Jesus. She closed her eyes and went to her glory. Dolly ran back into the room, and Mamma was gone.

No longer do we hear Mamma say, "Hey God!" But I know if God permits her to look down from heaven, she goes up to Him, a little four-foot-eleven woman, a little dynamo, and she says, "Hey God! Bless those people down below."

We depended so much on Mamma's prayers. My how we lived! Certain of every answer. Knowing that all we had to do was tell Mamma. "Mamma, please pray for my business. Mamma, please pray for this or pray for that." It was so inspiring, so encouraging in times of reversals, just to hear Mamma say, "Hey God! You see my boy. He need Your help. God, bless his business. Bless his home."

When the Lord took Mamma home, I had to learn to pray all over again. I had to learn to walk on my own feet. I had to learn to seek God on my own. Wherever I may be, driving down the highway, walking, in my office or my home, I follow the same pattern. I say, "Hey God! Listen, I want to talk to You." That's the way I talk to God now, the same way Mamma did it. Try it sometime. When you say, "Hey God!" you will feel His presence.

I get blessed in my soul every time I think about Mamma and our family and her tremendous outreach for Jesus Christ. She had such simplicity, such reality, such sincerity. God made Himself so real to our family. He proved Himself, showed His strength, His miracles. How could we help but believe? God showed us that salvation was real, the Holy Spirit and deliverance were real. Praise God! He is the same today as in those days when the 120 met in the Upper Room, the same now as the day the Pentecostal family brought the blessings of God into our lives through the acceptance of

Jesus Christ as our Savior, repentance, and the infilling of the Holy Spirit. God hasn't changed a bit. He is just as real, just as benevolent, just as glorious, and just as precious.

God acts in His own time and way. He cannot be rushed. I was privileged to testify to God's timetable in the case of Clem Marone, my partner in the meat-processing business in Fontana. Shortly after my healing in 1957, the company was liquidated. Clem's father, Nick, returned to Cleveland. Clem, Mary Jo, and their two children moved to Honolulu, where Clem and Mary Jo went into the pizza business. She traveled from door to door peddling the pizzas. God prospered them, and they branched out into other fields.

Clem and I had not kept close contact, but in 1968, Julie and I, with several other couples, flew to Honolulu, where we renewed our acquaintance with Clem and Mary Jo. Surprisingly, Mary Jo bubbled over with enthusiasm for the Lord, giving every evidence that she had been saved and baptized in the Holy Spirit. Clem lacked his wife's enthusiasm, and he told us why.

One Sunday morning, shortly after the move to Honolulu, Mary Jo told Clem she wanted to go to church. He replied, "Go ahead."

"I want to go to your church with you."

That Sunday morning Clem and his family attended the Assembly of God church. The pastor preached a salvation message. Mary Jo and the two children answered the altar call. They were saved and filled with the Holy Spirit. Praise the Lord! It was an answer to Clem's prayers, Mamma's prayers and the prayers of many others, including Clem's father, Nick.

"I just don't understand it," Clem complained. "I have been seeking the baptism in the Holy Spirit since 1957, and nothing has happened. Look at my wife. One altar call, and she gets the whole thing, saved and filled."

Julie and I and some other couples attending the convention laid hands on Clem and prayed for him. Soon he began to quiver like a reed in a windstorm. He broke forth in tongues. Praise God! Clem received such an infilling of the Holy Spirit that we thought he would burst, praising God for "oceans of blessings."

God is not a small God. Ask and believe and you will receive. Jesus told His apostles in John 15:7, "If ye abide in me, and my words abide in you, ye shall ask what ye will, and it shall be done unto you."

Continuing in John 15:1,2, 4-6: "I am the true vine, and my Father is the husbandman. Every branch in me that beareth not fruit he taketh away: and every branch that beareth fruit, he purgeth it, that it may bring forth more fruit. Abide in me, and I in you. As the branch cannot bear fruit of itself, except it abide in the vine; no more can ye, except ye abide in me. I am the vine, ye are the branches: He that abideth in me, and I in him, the same bringeth forth much fruit: for without me ye can do nothing."

Praise God! Amen!

Mamma and Dad Foglio

All correspondence may be mailed to:
Frank Foglio / P.O. Box 22057 / San Diego, CA. 92122